101 Socks

Circular Needles, Felted, Addi-Express, Toe Up, Crocheted, and Spiral Knit

Schiffer Publishing Ltd

4880 Lower Valley Road • Atglen, PA 19310

101 SOCKS

Published by Schiffer Publishing, Ltd.
4880 Lower Valley Road
Atglen, PA 19310
Phone: (610) 593-1777; Fax: (610) 593-2002
E-mail: Info@schifferbooks.com

For our complete selection of fine books on this and related subjects, please visit our website at www. schifferbooks.com. You may also write for a free catalog.

This book may be purchased from the publisher. Please try your bookstore first.

We are always looking for people to write books on new and related subjects. If you have an idea for a book, please contact us at proposals@schifferbooks.com.

Schiffer Publishing's titles are available at special discounts for bulk purchases for sales promotions or premiums. Special editions, including personalized covers, corporate imprints, and excerpts can be created in large quantities for special needs. For more information, contact the publisher.

Design: Gundula Zehner-Varga, Kathrin Rogg

Pattern Designs: Anja Lindner (p. 99), Babette Ulmer (pp. 32, 95, 98), Beate Meuser (p. 65), Christel Hurst (pp. 80, 81, 84), Gundula Steinert (pp. 108, 109), Heide Zuschke (pp. 10, 11, 42), Inge Dams (pp. 65, 80), Janne Graf (pp. 29, 36, 43, 94), Jessica von Felsch (pp. 113, 114), Junghans (p. 40), Käte Stödter (p. 135), Laila Wagner (pp. 134, 137, 139), Lana Grossa (pp. 115, 126, 127), Monika Ludwig (p. 60), Schachenmayr (p. 47), Sabine Schidelko (pp. 76, 77, 81), Simone Nägeli (pp. 28, 33), P. Haberland (pp. 114, 122), Veronika Hug (pp. 37, 50, 51, 56, 57, 60, 61, 64, 69, 72, 73, 84, 85, 114, 115, 122, 123), Waltraud Grund (pp. 108, 109, 113, 114), Ursula Remensperger (pp. 18, 19), Sabine Ruf (pp. 14, 15), Schoeller & Stahl (pp. 22, 23)

Styling: Almaz Werner-Tekeste (p. 11), Christine Oesterle (p. 29), Elke Reith (pp. 43, 60, 64, 65, 71, 72, 73, 76, 77, 94, 98, 99, 102, 108, 109, 113, 114, 118, 119, 122, 123), Ilka Baumgartner (p. 33), Betina Pohl (p. 46), Karin Schlag (pp. 28, 32, 37, 42, 50, 51, 55, 57, 60, 61, 64, 80, 81, 84, 85), Kirsten Galle (pp. 10, 42), Martina Schäfer (pp. 89, 95), Melanie Albisser (p. 135)

Photography: Wilfried Beege (p. 46), Christoph Läser (pp. 89, 95), Eberhard Schotte (p. 33), Erwin Wehinger (pp. 10, 28, 32, 42), Junghans (p. 40), Lana Grossa (pp. 115, 126, 127), Michael Steinert (pp. 69, 88, 103, 109), Petra Obermüller (pp. 11, 29), Rainer Muranyi (pp. 131, 132, 134, 139), Schachenmayr (p. 47), Uzwei Fotodesign (pp. 37, 42, 43, 50, 51, 56, 57, 60, 61, 64, 65, 69, 71, 73, 76, 77, 80, 81, 84, 85, 94, 98, 99, 102, 108, 109, 113, 114, 118, 119, 122, 123), Xandra M. Linsin (p. 135)

Library of Congress Control Number: 2014958595

Originally published as *101 Socken* by Christophorus Verlag GmbH & Co. KG, Freiburg, Germany, © Christophorus Verlag GmbH & Co. KG, 2013. Translated from the German by Carla Scott.

ISBN: 978-0-7643-4850-1
Printed in China

Dear Reader,

Seven techniques and 101 patterns make up a sock paradise! In these pages, you're sure to find the right technique and style for your feet.

Enjoy making and wearing your socks.

The Editors

In refined rounds

Use two circular needles to make the knitting go faster.

On your mark, get set, go!

Three different heels for the standard sock.

addi-Express Socks

The popular mini knitting machine can also make great socks.

Work them Toe Up!

Knit from the toe up, a sock can strike just the right mood.

Felting to feel good

Use the washing machine to create unique pieces.

Trends with a hook

Crocheted socks seduce even non-knitters.

Socks with the right spin

Spiral socks fit great even without a heel.

Contents

Crochet Abbreviations

ch	= chain
dc	= double crochet
rnd(s)	= round(s)
rep	= repeat
RS	= right side
sc	= single crochet
sp(s)	= space(s)
st(s)	= stitch(es)
tr	= treble crochet
WS	= wrong side
yo	= yarn over hook

What you should know about socks

A knitted sock is divided into different sections.

The cast-on edge is the start of the cuff. This edge can be designed with various types of cast-ons. The most common cast-on is described on the next page.

After the cast-on comes the cuff. It is usually elastic and knit in a ribbing pattern, which helps to keep the sock from slipping down the leg. But ruffles or other edges are also possible. The edgings are described in the respective pattern.

The leg comes directly after the cuff. It is the part of the sock that is mostly seen when worn with shoes. In addition to a Stockinette Stitch leg (only knit stitches) or a continuation of the cuff ribbing, another option this section lends itself to is a nice pattern stitch. Lace and cable patterns are very popular. If you're working a cable pattern be careful that the width of the leg is not too tight, as the cable stitches tend to pull in. You may need to increase above the cuff before starting the cable pattern, then decrease after the cables are complete. The leg is worked over the 1st and 4th needles, with the heel over the 2nd and 3rd needles. The heel should be as smooth and good-looking as possible. There are many different types of knitted heels. The most common are the Gusset Heel, the Heel Flap, and the Boomerang Heel. The heel is usually knit back and forth in rows. On pages 8–9, 26–27, and 40–41 you will find the steps for these different types of heels explained.

Since the heel gets the most wear, reinforcing it is recommended. This can be done by adding an auxiliary yarn, which is sometimes included in a sock yarn, and working particular pattern stitches. For a reinforced heel, in the 1st row, alternate 1 slip stitch with yarn in back and 1 knit stitch. In the 2nd row, work the stitches as knit the k sts and purl the p sts. Work the 3rd row same as the first, but begin with the knit stitch, to offset the pattern. In the 4th row work the stitches as knit the k sts and purl the p sts. Repeat these 4 rows for the heel pattern. The floats that appear on the wrong side of the work create a strong fabric.

The gusset merges the stitches of the back of the foot and the heel and decreases the stitches to the number needed for the foot. The foot refers to the section of the sock between the

heel and the beginning of the toe. Although this part of the sock would be large enough if using a smooth pattern, such as Stockinette Stitch, a more textured pattern may be a bit smaller and too tight around the foot. Therefore, the foot is usually knit in Stockinette stitch. The specifications for the required length are shown on the size charts on pages 142–143.

The tip of the sock ultimately encloses the toes. Again, there are various types of toes; the easiest is the Band Toe. The instructions for this type of toe can be found on page 9.

Mostly, socks are worked from the cuff to the tip of the toe. But more recently, it is popular to work them from the toe up. Instructions for these socks can be found in the chapter "From the Toe Up" (page 50).

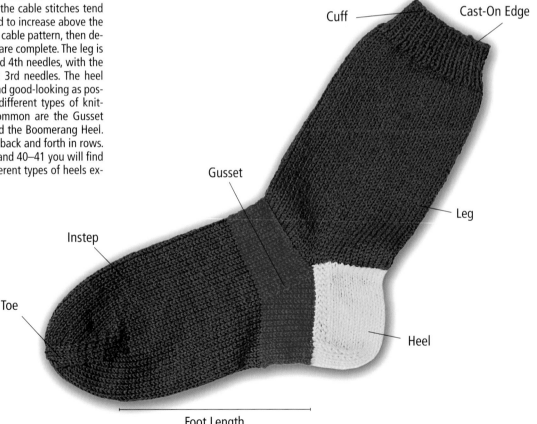

Cuff

Cast-On Edge

Gusset

Leg

Instep

Heel

Toe

Foot Length

The Cast-On

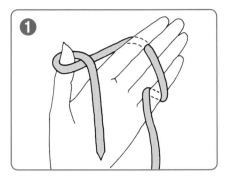

1 Wrap the end of the yarn around the left little finger, bring it between the index and middle finger, bring it to the back around the index finger and to the front. Then wrap around the thumb from front to back.

2 Hold both ends of yarn and insert right needle from below the loop on thumb. Bring the needle from back to front into the loop of the index finger and draw the yarn through…

3 … and pull the yarn through the loop on the thumb. Drop the yarn from thumb.

4 Using the thumb, grasp the end of the yarn from back to front, tighten the stitch and lift the thumb back up, etc.

5 Now the first two stitches are on the right needle. Insert the needle again from below the loop on thumb, pull through the yarn again and tighten the loop.

6 Each repeat of this represents a new stitch.

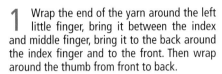

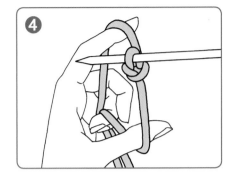

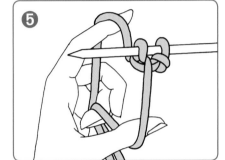

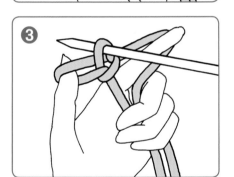

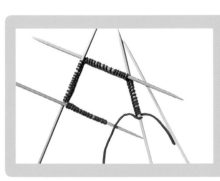

Dividing cast-on stitches over double-pointed needles

Divide the cast-on stitches evenly over the 4 double-pointed needles. The beginning of the round is the center back, between the 4th and 1st needle.

Basic Course for:
The Gusset Heel

Knitting socks with a Gusset Heel is a traditional art. Many of us have learned this method from our grandmothers.

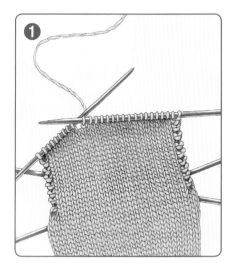

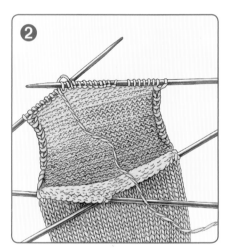

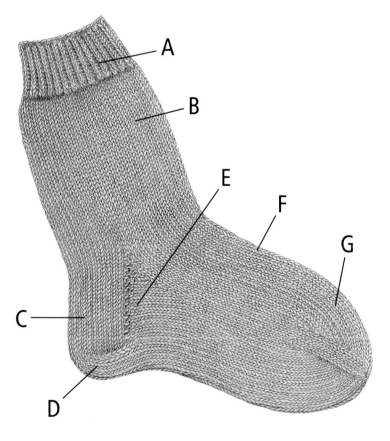

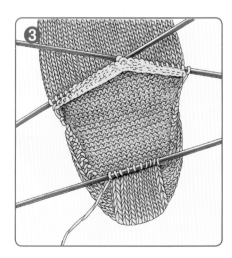

A = Cuff
B = Leg
C = Heel Flap, heel wraps back
D = Heel Cap, sits at the foot under the heel
E = Gusset, which is the transition between the heel and foot
F = Foot is knit back again on all 4 needles
G = Toe

Cast on stitches and divide evenly over 4 double-pointed needles. Place a yarn marker for the beginning of the round, which is always the center back and lies between the 4th and 1st needles.

Heel Flap: Place the stitches on the 2nd and 3rd needles on hold. Place the stitches on the 1st and 4th needles on one needle in order to work back and forth in rows, as indicated in each individual instruction.

❶ Heel Cap: Divide the stitches of the heel flap into 3 sections. Over the center third stitches work in Stockinette stitch or reinforced stitch as described on page 6. Then work the outer stitches as follows: On the right-side rows, always work the last stitch with the following stitch of outer left thirds as knit 2 together through back loops, turn and slip the first stitch purlwise.

❷ On the wrong-side rows, always work the last stitch with the following stitch of the outer right side as purl 2 together, turn and slip the first stitch knitwise.

❸ Gaps develop at the right and left of the center third stitches, making the beginning and end of the rows clearly visible. The decreases of cap are worked in this way until all the outer stitches are used up.

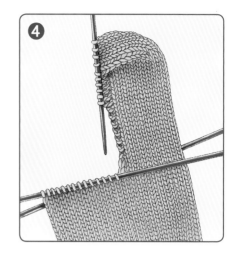

❹ Gusset: Continue to work in rounds over 4 needles. Divide the cap stitches in half over the 1st and 4th needles. With the 1st needle along the left edge of the heel flap, pick up 1 stitch over every 2 rows. Work the stitches on hold from the 2nd and 3rd needle. With the 4th needle along the right side of the heel flap, pick up 1 stitch over every 2 rows.

❺ In every 2nd round, on the 1st needle, knit the third and second to last stitches together, on the 4th needle knit the 2nd and 3rd stitches as SKP (= slip 1, knit 1, pass slipped stitch over knit 1). Repeat these decreases until there are the same number of stitches as before the heel shaping. For the foot, see the respective pattern instructions.

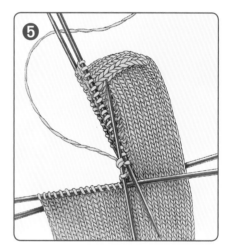

❻ Band Toe: On the 1st and 3rd needles always knit the 3rd and 2nd to last stitches together, on the 2nd and 4th needles always work the 2nd and 3rd stitches as SKP. Repeat these decreases every 2nd round until the stitch count is halved. Then repeat the decreases every round until 8 to 12 stitches remain. Draw a double strand of yarn through the stitches. Cut yarn and secure it.

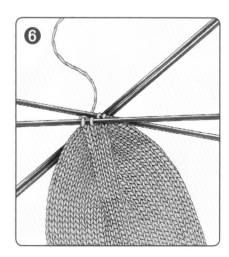

Taking a Walk in
Alpine Chic

Just right in natural colors from creamy white to beige to brown, these rustic socks and stockings are decorated with borders, cables, lace, and buttons.

Go all Alpine!

For all sock lovers who want to follow the trend from head to toe, in stores you can find great accessories in Heidi- or Edelweiss styles. Keep an eye out for cords or leather strips, which are perfect to use for laces. And appliqués and braid can make for stylish accents.

Rustic Socks
Size: Adult 10

Materials:
approx. 150 g natural (75% Wool, 25% Polyamide, 5% Acrylic, Yardage = 200 m/50 g), approx. 50 g dark brown (75% Wool, 25% Polyamide, Yardage = 125 m/50 g), 1 set (5) dpn size 3.5 mm (US 4)

Note: Work natural color double strand throughout!

Cable Pat: Rnd 1: *Purl 1, skip 1 st and knit the 2nd st in front of the first st, then knit first st and drop both sts from needle; rep from * around.
Rnd 2: *Purl 1, knit 2; rep from * around.
Rep rnds 1 and 2.
Stockinette Stitch (St st): Knit sts on RS rows, purl sts on WS rows.
Reverse Stockinette Stitch (Rev St st): Purl sts on RS rows, knit sts on WS rows.

Texture Pat: Work following the Stitch Chart.
Jacquard Border: Work in St st and Color Chart. When changing colors, carry color not in use loosely across back of work.

Gauge, over St st: 22 sts + 30 rows = 10 x 10 cm/4 x 4".

How to:
With natural cast on 48 sts (= 12 sts per needle) and work 12 rnds in Cable Pat. Then work as follows: 14 rnds Jacquard Border, then with natural, purl 1 rnd and knit 1 rnd, 10 rnds Texture Pat, knit 1 rnd and cont in Cable Pat. After 18 cm/7" from beg, change to dark brown and work Heel in Stockinette St, following Basic Course on pages 8–9. For the gusset, purl the corresponding sts tog. After the Heel work in natural working Rev St st over the sts of 1st and 4th needles and cont Cable Pat over the sts of the 2nd and 3rd needles. After 21 cm/8" from heel center, work the toe in St st and, work the decreases on the 3rd rnd, then every 2nd rnd 4 times, then every rnd.

Color Chart

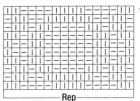

Rep

Stitch Chart

Stitch Key:
☐ = 1 k st
⊟ = 1 p st
☐ = natural
ⅹ = dark brown

Rep

1 square = 1 st + 1 rnd

Knee Socks
Size: Adult 7/8

Materials:
approx 100 g natural (41% Wool, 34% Cotton, 25% Polyamide, Yardage = 200 m/ 50 g), 1 set (5) dpn size 2.5 mm (US 1), 1 crochet hook size 3 mm (US D/3), 1 cable needle (cn), Elastic band 0.5 cm/½" wide, 2 round Horn buttons, 2 heart buttons, 4 horn rings

Stockinette Stitch (St st): Knit sts on RS rows, purl sts on WS rows; in rnds, knit every rnd
Garter st: Knit every row, in rnds alternate knit 1 rnd, purl 1 rnd.
Band Pat: 6 rnds St st, 1 rnd alternating k2tog and 1 yo, 6 rnds St st

Cable Pat: Work following the chart.

Gauge, St st: 30 sts and 42 rows = 10 x 10 cm/4 x 4".

How to:
Left Stocking: Cast on 72 sts (= 1st needle 12 sts, 2nd + 3rd needles 14 sts each, 4th needle 32 sts) and work Band Pat. On the next rnd knit each st together with the corresponding cast-on sts, up to the last 3 sts, knit the last 3 sts without joing to cast-on for openng for weaving in elastic. Then cont in Cable Pat. After 11 cm/4½" above band on an even-numbered rnd beg calf decreases. At the calf, work SKP (= slip 1 st knitwise, knit 1, pass slipped st over knit 1) with the 4th st and the following st and knit the 4th-to-last st tog with the previous knit st. Rep this decrease every 8th rnd twice more, every 6th rnd twice and every 4th rnd once. Then work SKP with the 2 sts before center calf every 4th rnd twice more and work k2tog with the 2 sts after the calf center = 56 sts. Work even until 29 cm/11½" above band. Over the 28 sts

on the 1st and 4th needles work the heel in St st following Basic Course on Pages 8–9. Work the outer 3 sts each side of heel flap in garter st and the gusset decreases every 3rd rnd. After the Heel sts. work the sts on 1st and 4th needles in St st, and over the sts of the 2nd and 3rd needles cont in Cable Pat, crossing the first 2 sts of the 2nd needle with the first 2 sts of the 3rd needle. After 18 cm/7" from heel center, work the toe in St st, work the decreases every 3rd rnd twice, every 2nd rnd 3 times, then every rnd.
Right Stocking: Work in reverse of Left Stocking.

Finishing:
Weave the elastic band through opening of the cuff band facing. Lay the heart button on the round button and sew to the center of the diamond. Crochet two double-strand chains each 12 cm/4¾" long, thread on the end of the horn rings, and knot. Fasten these cords around the buttons and secure in place.

Stitch chart

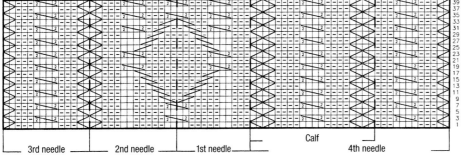

3rd needle — 2nd needle — 1st needle — Calf — 4th needle

Stitch Key:
☐ = 1 k st   ⊟ = 1 p st

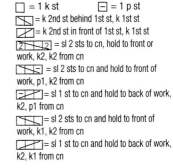
= k 2nd st behind 1st st, k 1st st
= k 2nd st in front of 1st st, k 1st st
= sl 2 sts to cn, hold to front or work, k2, k2 from cn
= sl 2 sts to cn and hold to front of work, p1, k2 from cn
= sl 1 st to cn and hold to back of work, k2, p1 from cn
= sl 2 sts to cn and hold to front of work, k1, k2 from cn
= sl 1 st to cn and hold to back of work, k2, k1 from cn

Only even-numbered rnds are shown. Work odd-numbered rnds as k the knit sts and p the purl.
Work rnds 1–40 once, then rep rnd 37–40.

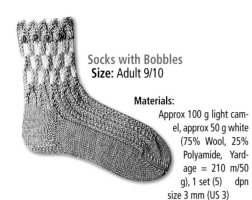

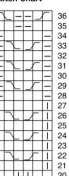

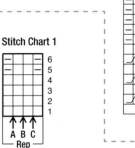

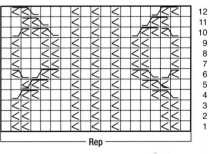

Socks with Bobbles
Size: Adult 9/10

Materials:
Approx 100 g light camel, approx 50 g white (75% Wool, 25% Polyamide, Yardage = 210 m/50 g), 1 set (5) dpn size 3 mm (US 3)

Cable Pat: Work following the chart.

Pattern Sequence: Work rnds 1–27 once, rep rnds 14–20 once, rnds 28–34 once, then cont to rep rnds 35+36. When changing colors, twist yarns on WS to prevent holes in work. Carry colors not in use loosely across back of work.

Stockinette Stitch (St st): Knit on RS rows, purl on WS rows; in rnds, knit every rnd.

Garter st: Knit every row.

Gauge, St st: 30 sts and 40 rows = 10 x 10 cm/4 x 4".

How to:
Cast on 60 sts in white (= 1st and 4th needles 14 sts each, 2nd + 3rd needles 16 sts each) and work in Cable Pat and Pat Sequence, working the 1st rnd in white, then cont in light camel. After 48 rnds from beg work the Heel in St st and light camel, following Basic Course on pages 8–9. Work the outer 3 sts each side of heel flap in garter st. After the Heel, work in light camel working the sts on 1st and 4th needles in St st and over the sts of the 2nd and 3rd needles cont in Cable Pat. After 20 cm/8" from heel center, work the toe in St st, working SKP (= slip 1 st knitwise, knit 1, pass slipped st over knit 1) with the 3rd and 2nd to last sts of the 1st and 3rd needles and work k2tog with the 2nd and 3rd sts of the 2nd and 4th needles. Work the first 2 decreases on the 2nd + 3rd needles, until there are 14 sts on needle.

Stitch Key:
- ☐ = 1 k st
- Ⅰ = 1 k st in white
- ⊟ = 1 p st
- = k 2nd st in front of 1st st, k 1st st
- = k 2nd st behind 1st st, k 1st st
- N = 1 bobble: work 4 sts in 1 st (= k1, yo, k1, yo), work 2 rows St st, then pass the 1st–3rd sts over the 4th st

Stitch Chart

Rep

Country House Socks
Size: Adult 10/11

Materials:
Approx 100 g camel, approx 50 g dark brown (75% Wool, 25% Polyamide, Yardage = 210 m/50 g), 1 set (5) dpn size 3 mm (US 3), 1 crochet hook size 3.5 mm (US E/4), 2 brown leather cords each 1.5 m/1.5yd long

Stockinette Stitch (St st): Knit sts on RS rows, purl sts on WS rows.
Waffle Pat: Follow Stitch Chart 1. Rep rnds 1–6.
Braid Pat: Follow Stitch Chart 2. Rep rnds 1–12.

Gauge, St st: 30 sts and 42 rnds = 10 x 10 cm/4 x 4".

How to:
Cast on 63 sts in camel, divide sts as follows: 1st needle: 15 sts Waffle Pat; 2nd needle: 7 sts, Waffle Pat from arrow A, the first 9 sts Braid Pat; 3rd needle: the last 10 sts Braid Pat, 7 sts Waffle Pat from arrow B; 4th needle: 15 sts Waffle Pat from arrow C. After 60 rnds from beg work the Heel in St st and follow Basic Course on pages 8–9. After the Heel sts work sts on 1st and 4th needles in Waffle Pat, work over the sts of the 2nd and 3rd needles as before. After 21 cm/8" from heel center work the toe in St st.

Finishing:
With crochet hook and dark brown, work around cast-on edge as follows: *1 sc, ch 5; rep from *, working sc in every st. Weave the leather cords through the Braid Pat, see photo.

Stitch Chart 1

6
5
4
3
2
1

↑ ↑ ↑
A B C
Rep

Stitch Key
- ☐ = 1 k st
- ◁ = 1 k st through back loop
- ⊟ = 1 p st
- = slip 2 sts to cn and hold to front of work, p1, k2 through back loop from cn
- = slip 1 st to cn and hold to back of work, k2 through back loop, p1 from cn
- = slip 2 sts to cn and hold to front of work, k1 through back loop, k2 through back loop from cn

Stitch Chart 2

12
11
10
9
8
7
6
5
4
3
2
1
Rep

- = slip 1 st to cn and hold to back of work, k2 through back lp, k1 through back loop from cn
- = slip 1 st to cn and hold to front of work, p1, k1 through back loop from cn
- = slip 1 st to cn and hold to back of work, k1 through back loop, p1 from cn

Winter-warm
Pattern Wonder

No more cold feet! Cuddly, warm socks for the entire family, with interesting patterns and original details. They make winter a pleasure!

Women's Socks with Cable-Bobble Edge
Size: Adult 8/9 (10/11)

Materials:
Approx 100 g purple (C) and approx 50 g lilac-green-blue mix (B) (80% Wool, 20% Polyamide, Yardage = 210 m/50 g), 1 set (5) dpn size 2.5 mm (US 1), crochet hook size 2.5 mm (US B/1), 1 Cable needle (cn), 4 purple buttons

Bobble Pat: multiple of 15 (16) sts: Work in rnds following Stitch Chart 1. Work the stitch rep 1 (2) times around. Work rnds 1–4 twice and rnds 1–3 once more.
Basketweave Pat: multiple of 6 sts: In rnds follow Chart 2. Work the stitch rep around. Work rnds 1–16 once, then rep rnds 2–9 once more.

Gauge, St st: 30 sts and 42 rnds/rows with 2.5 mm needles = 10 x 10 cm/4 x 4"

How to:
With 2.5 mm needles and C, cast on 60 (64) sts, divide sts evenly over 4 needles, join to work in rnds and for the picot edge, work 6 rnds St st, 1 eyelet rnd (= alternate k2tog, yo) and 6 rnds St st. Then for the cuff band, work 24 rnds of Basketweave Pat, inc 24 (26) sts evenly on the first rnd = 84 (90) sts. On the last Basketweave Pat rnd, dec 24 (26) sts evenly spaced around = 60 (64) sts. Then work 11 rnds in Bobble Pat. Change to B and cont in St st, dec 2 sts = 58 (62) sts. On the 1st and 4th needles there are 15 (16) sts each, on the 2nd and 3rd needles there are 14 (15) sts each. Work for 7 cm/2¾". Work the Heel Cap following the Basic Course on pages 8–9. Then pick up 15 (16) sts along each side of the heel and cont over all 68 (74) sts in St st. For the Instep decreases, knit the last 2 sts of 1st needle tog and work SKP over the first 2 sts of 4th needle, every 2nd rnd 5 (6) times = 58 (62) sts. After 15 (16) cm/6 (6¼)" from end of Heel, cont over all sts in St st and work the Toe following the instructions on page 9. Cut yarn and draw through remaining sts.

Finishing:
Fold picot rnd at beg of cuff to WS and sew in place. Make 2 twisted cords approx 40 cm/16" long with B. Weave the cords through the 2nd crossing rnd of Basketweave Pat, beginning and ending at the outer sides. Thread the cord ends through one button and knot the ends. Tie cords in a bow.

Stitch Chart 1

Stitch Chart 2

Stitch Key see page 17

Children's Socks with Pattern Edge

Size: Child 7½/8 (8/8½)

Materials:

Approx 100 g purple-red mix (80% Wool, 20% Polyamide, Yardage = 210 m/50 g), 1 set (5) dpn size 2.5 mm (US 1), crochet hook size 2.5 mm (US B/1), 1 Cable needle (cn)

Peacock Tail Pat: multiple of 11 sts: Work in rnds following Stitch Chart. Work the stitch rep around. Rep rnds 1 and 2.

Ribbing Pat: Knit 1, purl 1 ribbing.
Garter Stitch: Knit every row.

Gauge, St st: 30 sts and 42 rnds/rows with 2.5 mm needles = 10 x 10 cm/4 x 4".

How to:

Cast on 55 sts, divide sts evenly over 4 needles, join to work in rnds and for the cuff border work in Peacock Tail Pat. After 6 cm/2½", dec 5 (3) sts evenly around = 50 (52) sts. Work in Ribbing Pat over these sts. There are 13 (13) sts on 1st and 4th needles and 12 (13) sts on 2nd and 3rd needles. After ribbing measures 4 cm/1½", cont in St st for 4 cm/1½". Work the Heel Cap following the Basic Course on pages 8–9. Work the outer 2 sts of the heel flap in garter st. For the Instep decreases work k2tog with the last 2 sts of the 1st needle, and work SKP with the first 2 sts of 4th needles every 2nd rnd 4 times = 50 (52) sts. After 11 (11.5) cm/4¼ (4½)" from end of Heel, cont in St st for the Toe over all sts. Work the Toe following the Basic Course on page 9. Cut yarn, draw through rem sts and secure.

Finishing:

Crochet 2 chain cords each approx 28 cm/11" long, leaving long beginning and end strands hanging. With the end strands, make a bobble as follows: ch 4, in the 1st ch work 5 dc tog (= work each dc up to the last 2 loops, yo and draw through all loops on hook), ch 3, in the top of the 5 dc tog, work another 5 dc tog, work 1 slip st in the first ch. Cut yarn end and secure. Weave the cords through the front side of the sock, begin and end at the last rnd of the Peacock Tail Pat. With the beginning strand of the cord, make 1 bobble as before. Tie cords into a bow.

Stitch Chart

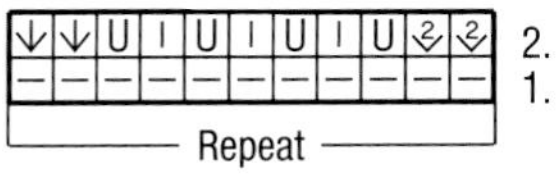
2.
1.
Repeat

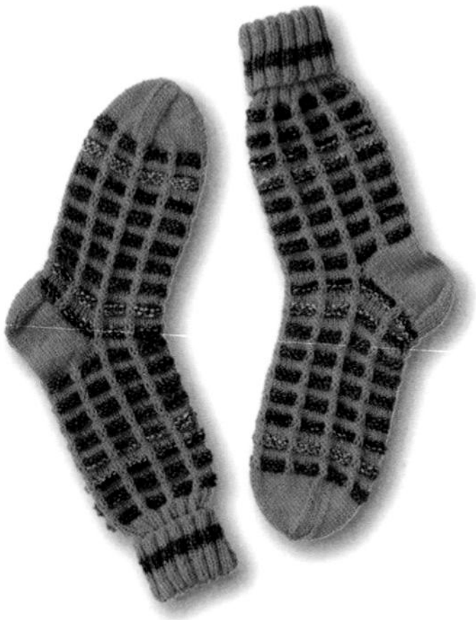

Children's Socks with Woven Pattern

Size: Child 6½/7 (7½/8)

Materials:

Approx 100 g pink (D) and approx 50 g purple mix (E) (80% Wool, 20% Polyamide, Yardage = 210 m/50 g), 1 set (5) dpn size 2.5 mm (US 1), crochet hook size 2.5 mm (US B/1, 1 Cable needle (cn)

Woven Pat: multiple of 7 sts: In rnds Follow the Stitch Chart. Work the stitch rep around. Rep rnds 1–8. The letters at the side of the chart represent the colors.
Ribbing Pat: Knit 2, purl 2 ribbing.

Gauge, St st: 30 sts and 42 rnds/rows with 2.5 mm needles = 10 x 10 cm/4 x 4".

How to:

With D cast on 48 (56) sts, divide sts evenly over 4 needles, join to work in rnds and for the cuff work in Ribbing Pat, working 1 cm/¼" in D, 1 cm/¼" in E and 8 cm/3¼" in D. On the last rib rnd, increase 1 (0) st = 49 (56) sts. Then work in Woven Pat for 11 (13) cm/4½ (5)" above rib band. Work the Heel Cap over the 12 (14) sts of 1st and 4th needles following the Basic Course on pages 8–9. Then pick 12 (14) sts along each side of heel edge and cont over all 57 (66) sts in Woven Pat, placing the sts of the Woven Pat so that the pat on the Instep continues as before. Also, work the 4 (5) sts on each side of the Instep without the Woven Pat. For the Instep, work k2tog with the last 2 sts of 1st needle and work SKP with the first 2 sts of 4th needle every 2nd rnd 4 (5) times = 49 (56) sts. Then cont Woven Pat over all sts as before. After 10 (13) cm/4 (5)" from end of Heel work over all sts in St st with D. Work the Toe following the Basic Course on page 9. Cut yarn draw through rem sts and secure.

Finishing:

Fold ribbed cuff in half to outside.

Stitch Chart

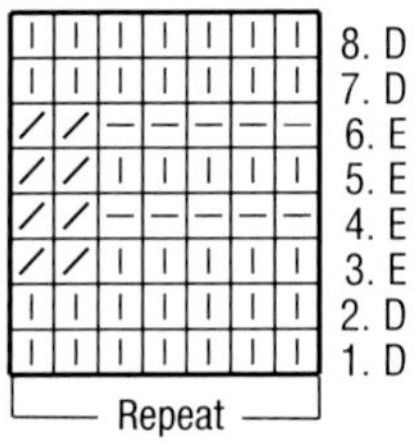
8. D
7. D
6. E
5. E
4. E
3. E
2. D
1. D
Repeat

Women's Socks in Half Brioche Rib Pattern
Size: Adult 9/10 (11/12)

Materials:
Approx 100 g purple-lilac-pink (65% Wool, 16% Polyamide, 15% Silk, 4% Cashmere, Yardage = 190 m/50 g), 1 set (5) dpn size 2.5 mm (US 1), crochet hook size 2.5 mm (US B/1), 1 cable needle (cn)

Half Brioche Rib: over an even number of sts: Rnd 1: *knit 1, purl 1; rep from *. Rnd 2: *Slip 1 st purlwise with yarn in front bringing yarn to back around needle to make a yo (called sl 1 with yo), purl 1; rep from *. Rnd 3: *Knit slip st and yo tog, purl 1; rep from *. Work rnds 1–3 once, then rep rnds 2 and 3.
Cable Cross: over 12 sts: slip 6 sts (beg with 1 knit st) to cn and hold to front of work, work the next 6 sts in Half Brioche Rib, then work the 6 sts from cn in Half Brioche Rib.

Gauge: 30 sts and 60 rnds/rows in Half Brioche Rib = 10 x 10 cm/4 x 4".

How to:
Cast on 60 (64) sts, divide sts evenly over 4 needles, join to work in rnds and for the cuff band work 7 cm/2¾" in Half Brioche Rib, then turn the work inside out and cont in Half Brioche Rib for another 7 cm/2¾". On the next (odd-numbered) rnd, work a Cable Cross over the 3rd–14th sts on the 1st and 3rd needles or the 2nd–13th (3rd–14th) sts of the 2nd and 4th needles. After 13 cm/5" from end of cuff band, work the Heel Cap following the Basic Course on pages 8–9, working the outer 2 sts in garter st. Then pick up 15 (16) sts along each side of the Heel and cont over all 70 (74) sts in Half Brioche Rib, working a Cable Cross on the inner half of the 2nd and 3rd needles every 7 cm/2¾" twice more. For the Instep decreases work k2tog over the last 3 sts of the 1st needle and work SKP with the first 2 sts on the 4th needle every 2nd rnd 5 times = 60 (64) sts. After 16 (17) cm/6¼ (6¾)" from end of Heel, cont over all sts in St St. Then work the Toe following instructions on page 9. Cut yarn and draw through rem sts and secure.

Finishing:
For the fringe, cut 3 strands each approx 4 cm/1½" for each fringe, and knot fringe in every 4th cast-on st on cuff. Fold cuff to outside.

Men's Socks in Gray
Size: Adult 10/11 (11/12)

Materials:
Approx 100 g gray (65% Wool, 16% Polyamide, 15% Silk, 4% Cashmere, Yardage = 190 m/50 g), 1 set (5) dpn size 2.5 mm (US 1), crochet hook size 2.5 mm (US B/1), 1 cable needle (cn)

Cable Pat: multiple of 8 sts: Work in rnds following the Stitch Chart. Only odd-numbered rnds are shown. Work even-numbered rnds as knit the k sts and purl the p sts. Work the stitch rep around; rep rnds 1–8.
Ribbing Pat: Knit 2, purl 2 ribbing.

Gauge, Cable Pat: 44 sts and 42 rnds/rows = 10 x 10 cm/4 x 4".

How to:
Cast on 64 sts, divide sts evenly over 4 needles, join to work in rnds and for the cuff band work 7 cm/2¾" in Ribbing Pat. Cont in Cable Pat, and on the 1st rnd inc 16 sts evenly spaced around = 80 sts. After 13 cm/5" above band work the Heel Cap following Basic Course on pages 8–9. On the 1st row dec 8 sts = 32 st and divide the sts as follows: 10-12-10. Then pick 17 sts along each side of Heel and cont over all 86 sts, working over the 46 sts of the 1st and 4th needles for the Sole in Ribbing Pat and for the Instep over the 40 sts of the 2nd and 3rd needles cont in Cable Pat, keeping to the Cable Pat as the sts left on hold for the Leg. For the Instep decreases, work k2tog over the last 3 sts of the 1st needle and work SKP with the first 2 sts on the 4th needle every 2nd rnd 6 times =74 sts. After 16 (17) cm/6¼ (6¾)" from end of inner half of Heel, on the 2nd and 3rd needles dec 10 sts evenly spaced around = 64 sts. Over these sts work in St st, then work the Toe following the instructions on page 9. Cut yarn, draw through rem sts and secure.

Stitch Chart

−	−	/	│	│	│	│	−	−	7.
│	│	−	−	│	│	│	│		5.
│	│	│	−	−	│	/	│	│	3.
−	│	│	│	│	│	│	−		1.

└─── Repeat ───┘

Stitch Key for Patterns on pages 15–17

│ = 1 knit st   − = 1 purl st

ᵁ = 1 yo

k2tog = k2tog

SKP = SKP: slip 1 st knitwise, knit 1, pass slipped st over knit 1

● = 1 bobble: work 5 sts in 1 st, then [turn work, purl 5, turn work, knit 5] twice, then pass the 4th, 3rd, 2nd and 1st st over the 5th st.

/ = slip 1 st knitwise, with yarn in back of work

= slip 2 sts to cn and hold to back of work, knit 2 and purl 2 from cn

= slip 2 sts to cn and hold to front of work, purl 2 and knit 2 from cn

3 ... 3 = slip 3 sts to cn and hold to back of work, knit 3 and purl 3 from cn

3 ... 3 = slip 3 sts to cn and hold to front of work, purl 3 sts and knit 3 from cn

Socks with Flair

End the boredom! Here are socks like you've never seen before. Knitted fringe, loops, cords, and multicolored border cables take these socks that extra mile.

Women's Socks with Buttons
Size: Adult 8/9 (10/11)

Materials:
Approx 50 g petrol (B), 100 g in natural (C), small amount each brown (A) and lilac (D) (75% Wool su-perwash, 25% Polyamide, Yardage = 420 m/100 g), 1 set (5) dpn size 2.5 mm (US 1), 2 mother-of-pearl-buttons, I-cord maker

Stockinette Stitch (St st): in rnds: Knit every rnd; in rows: Knit sts on RS rows, purl sts on WS rows.
Garter st: in rnds: Alternate knit 1 rnd, purl 1 rnd.

Gauge, Stockinette Stitch: 30 sts and 42 rows = 10 x 10 cm/4 x 4".

How to:
With in C, cast on 60 (62) sts, divide sts evenly over 4 needles, join to work in rnds (1st and 4th needles 15 (15) sts each, 2nd and 3rd needles (15/16) sts each and for the cuff band work 4 rnds in garter st. Cont in St st for another 11 cm/4½". Work the Heel Cap following Basic Course on pages 8–9. Work Heel and Cap in B and Foot in C. Then cont the Foot without decreases. After 15 (16) cm/6 (6¼)", work the Toe in B following instruction on page 9. Cut a long length, draw double strand through rem sts and secure.

Finishing:
For each sock, using I-cord maker, make 2 I cords each approx 21 (22) cm/8 (8½)" long in B and C, 1 cord each approx 21 (22) cm/8 (8½)" long in A and D and 1 cord approx 35 cm/14" long in B. Join beg and ends of all shorter cords together to make one long cord. Wrap the sewn cord around the top of the sock, following photo for placement, and sew in place. Tie the long B cord around the cuff and attach a button to end and knot the ends.

Women's Socks with Knitted Cords
Size: Adult 9/10 (11)

Materials:
Approx 100 g Petrol (B), 50 g lilac (D), a small amount of brown (A) (75% Wool superwash, 25% Polyamide, Yardage = 420 m/100 g), 1 set (5) dpn size 2.5 mm (US 1), I-cord maker

Garter st in rnds: Alternate knit 1 rnd, purl 1 rnd.
Gauge, Stockinette Stitch: 30 sts and 42 rows = 10 x 10 cm/4 x 4"
Stripe Pat: 10 rnds each in B, D, B, D and A.

How to:
With B, cast on 52 (54) sts, divide sts evenly over 4 needles, join to work in rnds (1st and 4th needles 13/13 sts each, 2nd and 3rd needles 13/14 sts each) and work in garter st and 50 rnds of Stripe Pat. Then work the Heel Cap following Basic Course on pages 8–9. Work the Heel, Cap and Foot in St st with B. On the 1st Heel row on the 1st and 4th needles as well as on the 1st Foot row on the 2nd and 4th needles, inc 2 sts, so that after the Instep decreases there are 60 (62) sts.

After 13.5 (14) cm/5¼ (5½)" from end of Heel, work another 2 cm/¾" in D, then work the Toe in B following instructions on page 9. Cut yarn, draw through rem sts and secure.

Finishing:
For each sock, using I-cord maker, make 2 cords each approx 25 cm/10" long in D as well as 1 approx 35 cm/14" long in A. Join beg and ends of two D cords together to make one long cord. Wrap the sewn cord around the top of the sock, and sew in place, with the extra length of each cord hanging to the outer side (see photo). Knot the ends of all cords. Tie the A and D cords in a knot (see photo).

Men's Socks with Braided Cord Edge
Size: Adult 10/11 (11/12) 14

Materials:
Approx 100 g brown (A), small amount each petrol (B) and natural (C) (75% Wool superwash, 25% Polyamide, Yardage = 420 m/100 g), 1 set (5) dpn size 2.5 mm (US 1), I-cord maker

Garter st in rnds: Alternate knit 1 rnd, purl 1 rnd.
3-st Cable: Rnd 1: Knit Rnd 2: Knit the 2nd and 3rd st behind the 1st st through the back loop, but do not drop these sts from needle, knit the 1st st and drop all 3 sts from needle). Rep rnds 1 and 2.
Stockinette Stitch (St st): in rnds: Knit every rnd; in rows: Knit sts on RS rows, purl sts on WS rows.
Gauge, Stockinette Stitch: 30 sts and 42 rows =10 x 10 cm/4 x 4".

How to:
With A, cast on 64 (64) 68 sts, divide sts evenly over 4 needles, join to work in rnds and for the cuff band work 4 rnds in garter st. Then for the Leg work in pat as follows: *knit 2, work 3-st Cable, knit 6 (6) 7, work 3-st Cable, knit 2; rep from * around. After 14 cm/5½" above end of cuff band, follow the Basic Course on pages 8–9. Work the Heel and Cap in St st. On the following 3rd rnd, for the Instep decreases, work k2tog over the 3rd and 2nd to last st of the 1st needle, work SKP with the 2nd and 3rd sts of the 4th needle. Rep these decreases every 3rd row until there are the same number of sts as before the beginning of the Heel. Then continue the Foot without decreases.
For the Sole, over sts of the 1st and 4th needles, work St st, and for the Instep, over the center 32

(32) 34 sts of the 2nd and 3rd needles, cont the cable pat same as on the Leg. After 16 (17) 17.5 cm/6¼ (6½) 6¾" from end of Heel, work the Toe in St st following the instructions on page 9. Cut yarn, draw through rem sts and secure.

Finishing:
For each sock, using I-cord maker, make 1 cord each approx 27/27/28 cm/10½/10½/11" long with A, B and C. Braid the 3 cords and sew the beginning and end of the cords together. Sew braided cord to top of sock cuff.

Children's Socks with Knitted Fringe
Size: Child 6/6½ (7½/8) 9/9½

Materials:
Approx 50 g brown (A), small amount each petrol (B), natural (C) and lilac (D) (75% Wool superwash, 25% Polyamide, Yardage = 420 m/100 g), 1 Wonder Knitter with 6 needles, 1 set (5) dpn size 2.5 mm (US 1)

Ribbing Pat: Knit 1, purl 1 ribbing.
Stripe Pat: 4 rnds each in D, A, B, C, D and C.
Gauge, Stockinette Stitch: 30 sts and 42 rows = 10 x 10 cm/4 x 4".

How to:
With D, cast on 46 (50) 54 sts, divide sts evenly over 4 needles, join to work in rnds (1st and 4th needles 11 (12) 13 sts each needle, 2nd and 3rd needles 12

(13) 14 sts each needle) and for the cuff band work in Ribbing Pat and 24 rnds of Stripe Pat. Then work the Heel Cap in A following Basic Course on pages 8–9. On the following 3rd rnd for the Instep decreases work k2tog over the 3rd and 2nd to last st of the 1st needle, work SKP over the 2nd and 3rd sts of the 4th needle. Rep these decreases every 3rd rnd until there are the same number of sts as before the beginning of the Heel. Then work the Foot without decreases in St st with A. Work the Toe after 9 (11) 13 cm/3½ (4½) 5" from end of Heel, following the instructions on page 9. Cut yarn, draw through rem sts and secure.

Finishing:
With the Wonder Knitter make a knitted cord approx 80 cm/31½" long in B and D. Divide the cords into 8 sections of equal lengths. On each section, tie a knot to mark the cutting edge to keep the sts

from unraveling and cut the cord just below the knot. Then make a 2nd cut so that each piece is approx 5 cm/2" in length. Sew these open sts to the top of cuff edge, alternating colors B and D.

Children's Socks with Loops
Size: Child 6½/7 (8/8½) 9/9½

Materials:
Approx 50 g each petrol (B) and natural (C), small amount lilac (D) (75% Wool superwash, 25% Polyamide, Yardage = 420 m/100 g), 1 set (5) dpn size 2.5 mm (US 1), I-cord maker

Garter st in rnds: Alternate knit 1 rnd, purl 1 rnd.
3-st Cable: Rnd 1: Knit Rnd 2: Knit the 2nd and 3rd st behind the 1st st through the back loop, but do not drop these sts from needle, knit the 1st st and drop all 3 sts from needle). Rep rnds 1 and 2.
Gauge, Stockinette Stitch: 30 sts and 42 rows = 10 x 10 cm/4 x 4".

How to:
With in D, cast on 48 (52) 56 sts, divide sts evenly over 4 needles, join to work in rnds and for the cuff

band work 4 rnds garter st. Then for the Leg work in C as follows: *knit 2, work 3-st Cable, knit 2 (3) 4, work 3-st Cable, knit 2; rep from * around. After 6 cm/2½" above end of cuff band, work the Heel Cap following Basic Course on pages 8–9. Work the Heel and Cap in Stockinette St.
Then for the Sole work in Stockinette Stitch over the sts of the 1st and 4th needles and for the Instep over the center 24 (26) 28 sts of the 2nd and 3rd needles cont in pat as for Leg. After 10 (11.5) 13 cm/4 (4½) 5" from end of Heel, work the Toe in Stockinette Stitch and B following the instructions on page 9. Cut yarn, draw through rem sts and secure.

Finishing:
Using I-cord maker, make 2 cords each approx 155 cm/61" long in B. Make loops of varying lengths from approx 4.5–6 cm/1¾–2½" and sew to top of Leg band.

Spring Fresh!

Soft natural tones and strong blue and green shades are especially suitable sock colors for spring. For children, there are socks with vibrant stripe combinations—and for adults, there's fresh experimenting with cable patterns.

Women's Socks with Two-Color Cable Pattern
Size: Adult 8/9 (10/11)

Materials:
50 g each sand mix (A) and turquoise (B) (75% Wool, 25% Polyamide, Yardage= 210 m /50 g), 1 set (5) dpn size 2.5 mm (US 1), crochet hook size 2.5 mm (US B/1), 1 Cable needle (cn)

Two-Color Cable Pat: multiple of 12 sts: In rnds, follow Stitch Chart. The letters at the side of the chart represent the colors. Work the stitch rep around. Work rnds 1–34 once, then work rnds 3–18 once more.
Stripe Pat: *2 rnds each in A and B; rep from *.
Ribbing Pat: Knit 1, purl 1 ribbing.
Gauge, Stockinette Stitch: 30 sts and 42 rows = 10 x 10 cm/4 x 4"

How to:
With 2.5 mm needles and B, cast on 60 sts, divide sts evenly over 4 needles, join to work in rnds and for the Rolled Edge work 2 cm/¾" in Stockinette St, then for the cuff band work in Ribbing Pat with A. After 2.5 cm/1", work 8 cm/3¼" = 50 rnds in Two-Color Cable Pat, and on the last rnd, inc 0 (4) sts at the inner half of the garter st section = 60 (64) sts. Then work Heel Cap in A following the instructions on pages 8–9. Then pick up 15 (16) sts along each side of the Heel and work over all 70 (76) sts in Stripe Pat, working Reverse Stockinette

Stitch over the 1st and 4th needles for the Sole, and Stockinette Stitch over the 2nd and 3rd needles for the Instep. For the Instep decreases, work k2tog over the last 2 sts of the 1st needle, work SKP over the first 2 sts of the 4th every 2nd rnd 5 (6) times = 60 (64) sts. After 14.5 (16) cm/5¾ (6¼)" from end of Heel, cont in Stockinette Stitch with A over all sts and work the Toe following the instructions on page 9. Cut yarn, draw through rem sts and secure.

Stitch Chart

Repeat

Women's Socks with Two-Color Cable Band
Size: Adult 9/10 (11)

Materials:
50 g each sand mix (A) and green (C) (75% Wool, 25% Polyamide, Yardage= 210 m /50 g), 1 set (5) dpn size 2.5 mm (US 1), crochet hook size 2.5 mm (US B/1), 2 cable needles (cn)

Two-Color Cable Band: Worked over 16 sts back and forth in rows following the Stitch Chart. The letters at the side of the chart represent the colors. Work rows 1–22 once, then rep rows 3–22.
Stripe Pat: *Work 2 rnds each in A and C; rep from *.
Ribbing Pat: Knit 2, purl 2 Ribbing.
Gauge, Stockinette Stitch: 30 sts and 42 rows = 10 x 10 cm/4 x 4"

How to:
With 2.5 mm needles and C, cast on 16 sts. For the Two-Color Cable Band work following the chart. After 20.5 cm/8" = 122 rows, bind off. Sew cast-on and bound-off edges tog. Then with 2.5 mm needles and A, along one side edge of the Cable Band, pick up 60 (64) sts, divide sts evenly over 4 needles, join to work in rnds and for the Leg work in Ribbing Pat for 8 cm/3¼". Work the Heel Cap with A, following the instructions on pages 8–9. Then pick up 15 (16) sts along each side of Heel and cont

in Stripe Pat over all 70 (76) sts, working in Reverse Stockinette St over of the 1st and 4th needles for the Sole, and Stockinette Stitch over the 2nd and 3rd needles for the Instep. For the Instep decreases work k2tog over last 2 sts of the 1st needle, work SKP over the first 2 sts of the 4th needle every 2nd rnd 5 (6) times = 60 (64) sts. After 15.5 (17.5) cm/6 (7)" from end of Heel, work the Toe with A.

Stitch Chart

Stitch Key for Patterns on Pages 24/25

⊞ = 1 selvage st   □ = 1 knit st   ⊟ = 1 purl st

◪ = slip 1 st purlwise, with yarn in back of work

◪ = slip 1 st knitwise, with yarn in front of work

Ⓤ = 1 yo
② = k2tog
◩ = SKP: slip 1 st knitwise, knit 1, pass slipped st over knit 1

⬚⬚② = slip 1 st to cn and hold to front of work, then knit 2 and k1 from cn.

◤◥ = slip 2 sts to cn and hold to front of work, slip 2 sts to 2nd cn and hold to back of work, slip 2 sts purlwise, with yarn in back of work, then knit the 2 sts from 2nd cn, then slip the 2 sts from 1st cn purlwise, with yarn in back of work.

⬚⬚◥ = slip 2 sts to cn and hold to back of work, slip 2 sts purlwise, with yarn in back of work, then knit 2 sts from cn

◤⬚⬚ = slip 2 sts to cn and hold to back of work, knit 2, then slip 2 sts from cn purlwise, with yarn in back of work.

◤⬚⬚ = slip 2 sts to cn and hold to front of work, knit 2, then slip 2 sts form cn purlwise, with yarn in back of work

⬚◥ = slip 2 sts to cn and hold to front of work, slip 2 sts purlwise, with yarn in back of work, then knit 2 from cn.

③ = insert needle into each of the 3 underlying yo's and draw up a loop to corresponding height.

◺◿ = Purl the 6 loops on needle together with the sts in between.

□ = No stitch, this square has no meaning, skip over it.

Men's Socks
Size: Adult 11/12 (15)

Materials:
Approx 100 g sand mix (75% Wool, 25% Polyamide, Yardage= 210 m /50 g), 1 set (5) dpn size 2.5 mm (US 1), crochet hook size 2.5 mm (US B/1), 1 Cable needle (cn)

Cable Pat: multiple of 6 sts: Work in rnds following the Stitch Chart. Work the stitch repeat around. Rep rnds 1–12.
Ribbing Pat: Knit 2, purl 2 Ribbing.
Gauge, Stockinette Stitch: 30 sts and 42 rows = 10 x 10 cm/4 x 4".

How to:
With 2.5 mm needles, cast on 64 (72) sts, divide sts evenly over 4 needles, join to work in rnds and for the cuff band work 3 cm/1¼" in Ribbing Pat. Cont in Cable

Pat, and on the 1st rnd inc 14 (12) evenly spaced = 78 (84) sts. There are 19 (21) sts each on 1st and 4th needles, 20 (21) sts each on the 2nd and 3rd needles. After 17 cm/6½" above band, dec 6 sts at the inner half of the 1st and 4th needles = 72 (78) sts. Then work the Heel Cap following the instructions on pages 8–9. Then pick up 16 (18) sts along each side of Heel and cont over all 84 (92) sts. Work Reverse Stockinette Stitch over the 44 (50) sts of the 1st and 4th needles for the Sole and cont Cable Pat over the 40 (42) sts of the 2nd and 3rd needles for the Instep, keeping the Cable Pat same as the Leg, and for size Adult 11/12, work the first and last 2 sts in Reverse Stockinette Stitch. For the Instep decreases, work k2tog over the last 2 sts of the 1st needle, work SKP over the first 2 sts of the 4th needle, every 2nd rnd 7 times = 70 (78) sts. After 17 (20) cm/6½ (8)" from end of Heel, cont in Stockinette Stitch over all sts and work the Toe following the instructions on page 9. Cut yarn and draw through rem sts.

Stitch Chart

Children's Striped Socks in Natural
Size: Child 7½/8 (8/8½)

Materials:
50 g each sand mix (A), turquoise (B) and green (C) (75% Wool, 25% Polyamide, Yardage= 210 m /50 g), 1 set (5) dpn size 2.5 mm (US 1), crochet hook size 2.5 mm (US B/1), 1 Cable needle (cn)

Openwork Pat: multiple of 10 sts: Work in rnds following the Stitch Chart. Work the stitch repeat around. Rep rnds 1–10.
Stripe Pat I: *6 rnds C, 4 rnds A, 6 rnds B, 4 rnds A; rep from *.
Stripe Pat II: * 2 rnds B, 4 rnds A, 2 rnds C, 4 rnds A; rep from *.
Gauge, Stockinette Stitch: 30 sts and 42 rows = 10 x 10 cm/4 x 4".

How to:
With 2.5 mm needles and B, cast on 50 sts, divide sts evenly over 4 needles, join to work in rnds and for the Rolled Edge work 1.5 cm/½" in Stockinette St, then for the cuff band work 1.5 cm/½" in Ribbing Pat and A. Then work 7 cm/2¾" = 30 rnds in Openwork Pat and Stripe Pat I, and on the last rnd, inc 1 st at the inner half on the 1st and 3rd needles = 52 sts. Then for the Heel work back and forth in rows in St st and A over the 13 sts of the 1st and 4th needles. When Heel measures 5.5 cm/2" work the Heel Cap following the instructions on pages 8–9. Then pick up 13 sts along each side of Heel and cont in St st and Stripe Pat II over all 60 sts. For the Instep decreases, work k2tog over the last 3 sts of the 1st needle and work SKP with the first 2 sts on the 4th needle every 2nd rnd 4 times = 52 sts.

After 10 (11.5) cm/4 (4½)" from end of Heel, cont. in St st and A over all sts and work the Toe following the instructions on page 9. Cut yarn draw through rem sts and secure.

Stitch Chart

Children's Striped Socks in Green
Size: Child 6½/7 (9/9½)

Materials:
50 g each sand mix (A), turquoise (B) and Green (C) (75% Wool, 25% Polyamide, Yardage= 210 m /50 g), 1 set (5) dpn size 2.5 mm (US 1), crochet hook size 2.5 mm (US B/1), 1 Cable needle (cn)

Slip St Pat: multiple of 4 sts: Work in rnds following the Stitch Chart. Work the stitch repeat around Rep rnds 1–12. The numbers at the side of the chart represent the colors.
Ribbing Pat: Knit 1, purl 1 ribbing.
Stripe Pat: *2 rnds A, 4 rnds B (C), 2 rnds A, 4 rnds C (B); rep from *.
Gauge, Stockinette Stitch: 30 sts and 42 rows = 10 x 10 cm/4 x 4".

How to:
With 2.5 mm needles and A, cast on 48 (56) sts, divide sts evenly over 4 needles, join to work in rnds and for the cuff band work 2 rnds each A, B and C in Ribbing Pat. Then with C work 1 eyelet rnd (= *yo, k2tog; rep from *) and 1 rnd Stockinette St. Cont in Slip St Pat for 6 cm/2½" = 26 rnds (7.5 cm/3" = 32 rnds). Work the Heel Cap following the instructions on pages 8–9. Then pick up 12 (14) sts along each side of Heel and cont in Stripe Pat over all 56 (66) sts, work in Reverse Stockinette Stitch over the 1st and 4th needles for the Sole, and Stockinette Stitch over the 2nd and 3rd needles for the Instep. For the Instep decreases, work k2tog over the last 2 sts of the 1st needle, work SKP over the first 2 sts of the 4th needle, every 2nd rnd 4 (5) times = 48 (56) sts. After 10 cm/4" = 42 rnds (13 cm/5" = 54 rnds) from end of Heel, cont in Stockinette Stitch with C (B) over all sts

Stitch Chart

and work the Toe following the instructions on page 9. Cut yarn, draw through rem sts and secure.

Basic Course for:
The Heel Flap

The rounded shape of the heel flap sits nicely on the foot. If reinforced, this heel is particularly durable.

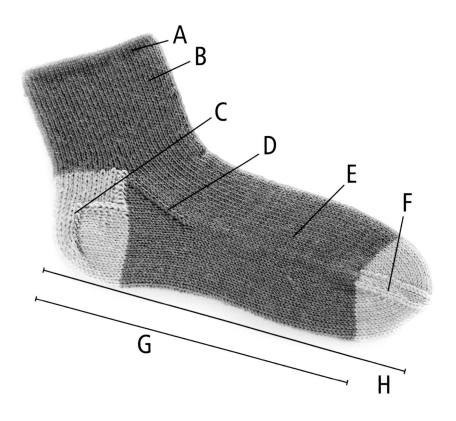

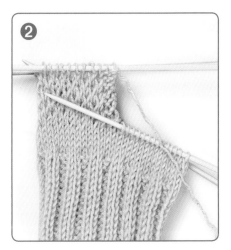

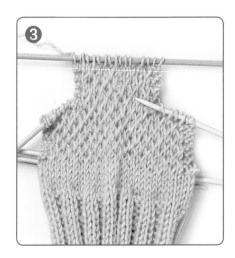

A = Cuff (Band, Rolled Edge, Turnback cuff, etc.)
B = Leg
C = Heel with 1st and 2nd Flaps
D = Gusset, which is the transition between the heel and foot
E = Foot, which is worked over all 4 needles
F = Toe
G = Foot length to beginning of Toe
H = Total foot length

❶ Place the stitches of the 1st and 4th needle on one needle and work back and forth in rows. The stitches of the 2nd and 3rd needles are on hold. The Heel Flap is worked in Stockinette Stitch (knit on RS row, purl on WS rows) or reinforced.

❷ At the same time the stitches at both outer edges of the heel are worked in garter stitch (knit every row), which facilitates the counting of rows and is distinctive. Work the number of rows as given on the Size Table on pages 126/127 until the 1st flap is complete. When this row number is reached, on the following row place the last stitches (see Size Table) on hold. On the wrong-side row, place the same number of stitches at the end of the row on hold.

❸ Over the remaining center stitches work in Stockinette stitch or reinforce (see page 9). Work the 2 outer stitches in garter stitch as before. Work the number of rows as given on the Size Table until the 2nd flap is complete. At end of the following row pick up 1 st in every 2 rows along the selvage edge.

❹ Work the stitches on hold from needle 2 and 3 together with the heel stitches as follows: on every 2nd row work SKP with the 1st stitch from st on hold. Turn, slip 1st stitch, purl the following stitches' links and then pick up the same number of stitches into the selvage stitches along the other side. Purl the last picked-up stitch together with the 1st stitch on hold.

Continue in Stockinette Stitch or reinforced stitch, working the decreases as before, until all the stitches on hold have been worked (for total rows see Size Table). On the next row, slip 1st stitch and knit half of the stitches (= stitches of the 4th needle).

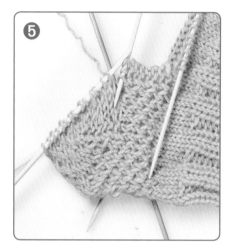

❺ Then continue to work in rounds. Redistribute the stitches over 4 needles as follows: The 2nd half of the heel stitches on the 1st needle, along the left edge of the 1st flap pick up 1 st in every 2nd row (= the number of pick up sts for the Gusset on the Size Table). Cont to work the sts on hold from the 2nd and 3rd needle. For the 4th needle along the right edge of the 1st flap pick up 1 st in every 2nd row (= picked up sts for Gusset) and the 1st half of the heel sts also on the 4th needle.

❻ Then work the Gusset. For the gusset decreases, on every 2nd round, on the 1st needle work the third and second to last sts as k2tog, on the 4th needle work the second and third sts as SKP (slip 1 stitch, knit 1, pass slipped stitch over, knit 1). Repeat these decreases until the number of stitches on the 1st and 4th needles is the same number as on the 2nd and 3rd needles. Then knit the foot to the specified length.

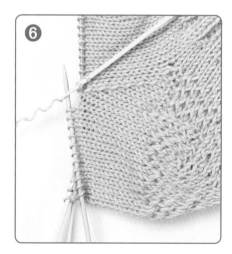

Tip
There are studs and rhinestones to iron on, or grommets and eyelets are available along with the simple tools you need to install them. This lets you easily spice up your socks as desired.

Sparkle and Glitter

Texture Pattern or Stockinette Stitch—the choice is yours. The short, single-color sock always looks great. Very creative and stylish, with small highlight studs, eyelets, and rhinestones.

Cuffed Socks
Size: Adult 8/9 (9/10)

Materials:
Approx 100 g purple (75% Wool, 18% Polyamide, 7% Acrylic, Yardage = 190 m/50 g), 1 set (5) dpn size 2.5 mm (US 1), 16 Star studs 10 mm in diameter, 16 clear rhinestones with setting

Band Pat: Knit 1, purl 1 ribbing
Stockinette Stitch (St st): Knit sts on RS rows, purl sts on WS rows.
Purl Garter St: Worked in rnds, alternate purl 1 rnd and knit 1 rnd.

Ribbing Pat: Work following the chart.

Gauge, Stockinette Stitch: 30 sts and 42 rows = 10 x 10 cm/4 x 4".

How to:
Cast on 64 sts over 4 needles (= 16 sts per needle) and for the cuff work 3 rnds Purl Garter St, 5 rnds Stockinette Stitch and 15 rnds Ribbing Pat. Then knit 1 rnd, work k2tog at end of each needle = 60 sts (= 15 sts per needle). Then work 16 rnds Band Pat and 7 rnds Stockinette St, then work the Heel Flap with reinforced Heel following the Basic Course on pages 26–27. After the Heel, cont in Stockinette st and when the foot measures 18.5 (19.5) cm/7¼ (7¾)", work the Star Toe (see page 140).

Finishing:
Decorate the Cuff and fold to outside. At the end of each short rib sew on 1 rhinestone and at the end of each long rib, iron on 1 star stud following the manufacturer's instructions.

Stitch Chart

>		>				15
>		>				14
>		>				13
>		>				12
>		>				11
>		>				10
>		>				9
>		>				8
>		>				7
>		>				6
>						5
>						4
>						3
>						2
>						1

Repeat

Stitch Key
☐ = 1 knit st
▷ = 1 purl st through back loop

Studded Socks
Size: Adult 8/9 (9/10)

Materials:
Approx 100 g turquoise wool-blend yarn (Yardage = approx 190 m/50 g), 1 set (5) dpn size 2.5 (US 1), 8 round iron-on studs 8 mm in diameter

Ribbing Pat: Knit 1, purl 1 ribbing
Stockinette Stitch (St st): Knit sts on RS rows, purl sts on WS rows.

Texture Pat: Work following the chart. Rep rnds 1–20.

Gauge, Stockinette Stitch: 30 sts and 42 rows = 10 x 10 cm/4 x 4".

How to:
Cast on 60 sts over 4 needles (= 15 sts per needle) and for the cuff band work 3 rnds in St st and 5 rnds in Ribbing Pat, then cont in Texture Pat for 23 rnds. Work Heel Flap with reinforced Heel following the instructions on pages 26–27. After the Heel, cont Texture Pat over the sts on the 2nd and 3rd needles, work in Stockinette Stitch over the sts on the 1st and 4th needle. When Foot measures 18.5 (19.5) cm/7¼ (7¾)", work Star Toe (see page 140).

Finishing:
In the squares on the Leg iron 1 stud following the manufacturer's instructions using photo as a guide or as desired.

Stitch Chart

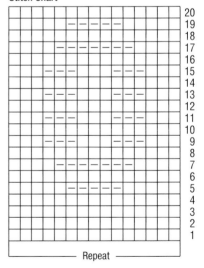

Repeat

Stitch Key
☐ = 1 knit st
— = 1 purl st

Blue Socks
Size: Adult 8/9 (9/10)

Materials:
Approx 100 g blue (75% Wool, 18% Polyamide, 7% Acrylic, Yardage = 190 m/50 g), 5 g auxiliary yarn for reinforcing the Heel, 1 set (5) dpn size 2.5 mm (US 1), 12 green rhinestones with setting

Stockinette Stitch (St st): Knit sts on RS rows, purl sts on WS rows.
Purl Garter St: in rnds alternate purl 1 rnd and knit 1 rnd.
Diamond Pat: Follow Stitch Chart 1.
Dot Pat: Follow Stitch Chart 2. Rep rnds 1–8.

Gauge, Stockinette Stitch: 30 sts and 42 rows = 10 x 10 cm/4 x 4".

How to:
Cast on 60 sts over 4 needles (= 15 sts per needle) and for the Leg work as follows: 8 rnds St st, 4 rnds Purl Garter st, 3 rnds St st, 9 rnds Diamond Pat, 3 rnds St st and 3 rnds Purl Garter st. Then work the Heel Flap with reinforced Heel following the instructions on pages 26–27. After the Heel work in Dot Pat over the sts on the 2nd and 3rd needles and St st over the sts on the 1st and 4th needles. When Foot measures 18.5 (19.5) cm/7¼ (7¾)", work Star Toe (see page 140) .

Finishing:
Sew 1 rhinestone in the diamonds on the Leg.

Stitch Chart 1

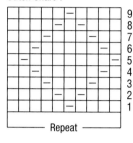

Stitch Chart 2

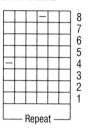

Socks with Lacing
Size: Adult 8/9 (9/10)

Materials:
Approx 100 g Jeans (80% Wool, 20% Polyamide, Yardage = 210 m/50 g), 1 set (5) dpn size 2.5 mm (US 1), 2 packages grommets and star studs if desired, approx 2 m/2 yd silver rayon cord

Garter st: in rnds alternate knit 1 rnd and purl 1 rnd.
Stockinette Stitch (St st): Knit sts on RS rows, purl sts on WS rows.

Gauge, Stockinette Stitch: 30 sts and 42 rows = 10 x 10 cm/4 x 4".

How to:
Cast on 60 sts over 4 needles (= 15 sts per needle) and for the cuff band work 6 rnds garter st, then cont in St st. After 14 rnds above band for the front slit, bind off the sts on the 2nd and 3rd needles, and work 3 rows St st over remaining sts, then cast on sts over the bound-off sts on next row and cont to work in rnds. After 32 rnds above band, work the Heel Flap with reinforced Heel following the instructions on pages 26–27. When foot length measures 18.5 (19.5) cm/7¼ (7¾)" work Star Toe (see page 140).

Finishing:
Attach 12 grommets evenly spaced on the top and bottom half of the slit following the instructions on the package, then weave the cord through the grommets and tie in a bow, see photo. Attach 1 star stud to outer cuff band.

Colorful
Summer Hits

These colorful socks in large and small are just the thing to wear while walking the boardwalk. The gradients come directly from the yarn, and are combined with heels and toes in a solid color. Pompons, fringe, and knitted cords add decoration.

Socks with Fringe
Size: Child 9/9½ (Adult 7/8)

Materials:
Approx 100 g blue-orange-yellow self-striping yarn

(75% Wool, 25% Polyamide, Yardage = 210 m/50 g), approx 50 g each yellow and violet (75% Wool, 25% Polyamide, Yardage = 210 m/50 g), 1 set (5) dpn size 2.5 mm (US 1)

Stockinette Stitch (St st): Knit sts on RS rows, purl sts on WS rows.

Gauge, Stockinette Stitch: 30 sts and 42 rows = 10 x 10 cm/4 x 4".

How to:
Cast on 56 sts with yellow over 4 needles (= 14 sts per needle) and work in St st as foll: 4 cm/1½" in yellow, 2 cm/¾" in violet and 4 cm/1½" in blue-orange-yellow. Then work the Heel Flap in yellow with reinforced Heel following Basic Course on pages 26–27. After the Heel, cont in St st in blue-orange-yellow and when foot length measures 16 (17.5) cm/6¼ (7)", work Star Toe (see page 140) in violet.

Finishing:
Attach 5 fringe (= using 4 strands 14 cm/5½" long for each fringe) to outer Leg on the last yellow rnd and 3 sts apart. Alternate 1 fringe in yellow, violet, blue-orange-yellow, violet and yellow.

Socks with Wavy Edge
Size: Child 9/9½ (Adult 7/8)

Materials:
Approx 100 g blue-orange-yellow self-striping yarn (75% Wool, 25% Polyamide, Yardage = 210 m/50

g), approx 50 g each yellow and green (75% Wool, 25% Polyamide, Yardage = 210 m/50 g), 1 set (5) dpn size 2.5 mm (US 1), 1 ADDI- crochet hook size 2.5 mm (US B/1)

Stockinette Stitch (St st): Knit sts on RS rows, purl sts on WS rows.
Scallop Edge: Rnd 1: *knit 8, bring yarn from under the cast on edge and draw up a long loop on the right needle; rep from *.
Rnd 2: Knit all sts, knitting the loop made in rnd 1 together with the following st.

Gauge, Stockinette Stitch: 30 sts and 42 rows = 10 x 10 cm/4 x 4".

How to:
With yellow, cast on 56 sts onto 4 needles (= 14 sts per needle) and work in St st as follows: 2 rnds in yellow, 4 rnds in blue-orange-yellow, 2 rnds Scallop

Edge and 2 rnds St st in green, 4 rnds in blue-orange-yellow, 5 rnds in yellow and 6 rnds in blue-orange-yellow. Then work the Heel Flap in green with reinforced Heel following Basic Course on pages 26–27. After the Heel cont in St st working 1 rnd in green and 5 rnds in blue-orange-yellow, then cont in yellow. When Foot measures 15 (16.5) cm/6 (6½)", work 4 rnds in blue-orange-yellow, then work Star Toe (see page 140) in green.

For the Flower: Rnd 1: With crochet hook and yellow, ch 4, join with sl st to first ch to form ring. Rnd 1: Ch 1, work 10 sc in ring, join with sl st to beg ch. Rnd 2: With blue-orange-yellow, ch 1, work 2 sc in each st, join rnd with sl st. Make 2 Flowers. Sew on flowers to cuff.

Socks with Pompons
Size: Child 9/9½ (Adult 7/8)

Materials:
Approx 100 g pink-yellow-blue self-striping yarn (75% Wool, 25% Polyamide, Yardage = 210 m/50 g) approx 50 g each turquoise and mango (75% Wool, 25% Polyamide, Yardage = 210 m/50 g), 1 set (5) dpn size 2.5 mm (US 1)

Stockinette Stitch St st: Knit sts on RS rows, purl sts on WS rows.
Reverse Stockinette Stitch (Rev St st): in rnds, purl every rnd.

Gauge, Stockinette Stitch: 30 sts and 42 rows = 10 x 10 cm/4 x 4".

How to:
With Mango cast on 56 sts over 4 needles (= 14 sts per needle) and work as follows: 2 cm/¾" each Rev St st in Mango, St st in pink-yellow-blue, Rev St st in turquoise and 1 cm/¼" St st in pink-yellow-blue. Then work the Heel Flap in Mango with reinforced Heel following Basic Course on pages 26–27. After the Heel, cont in St st in pink-yellow-blue and when the Foot measures 16 (17.5) cm/6¼ (7)", work Star Toe (see page 140) in turquoise following the Basic Course.

Finishing:
Make 4 pompons each using Mango and turquoise with a 4 cm/1½" finished diameter and sew to the center knit stripe on the Leg, alternating colors.

Sneaker Socks with Rolled Edge
Size: Adult 9/10

Materials:
Approx 100 g Sock Wool blue-green-yellow self-striping yarn (75% Wool, 25% Polyamide, Yardage approx 210 m/50 g), 50 g or small amount blue, 1 set (5) dpn size 2.5 mm (US 1)

Stockinette Stitch (St st): Knit sts on RS rows, purl sts on WS rows; in rnds knit every rnd.

Gauge, Stockinette Stitch: 30 sts and 42 rows = 10 x 10 cm/4 x 4".

How to:
With blue, cast on 60 sts and for the Rolled Edge work 8 rnds in St st. Then cont in St st with self-striping yarn for 2 cm/¾". Work reinforced Heel Flap following the Basic Course on pages 26–27. Then cont in St st and work the Foot for approx 20.5 cm/8". Work the Toe in St st following Basic Course on page 9.

Tip
In order to have both socks the same color striping, beg the yarn at the same color section for both socks.

Maritime
Sock Dreams

Bright blue and cool white, combined with crisp cable patterns: the elements of the ever-stylish nautical look. Try upping their elegance with glittery touches.

Socks with Cable Cuff
Size: Adult 8/9 (9/10)

Materials:
Approx 100 g light blue, approx 50 g each bright white and medium blue (80% Wool, 20% Polyamide, Yardage = 210 m/50 g), 1 set (5) dpn size 2.5 mm (US 1), 1 Cable needle (cn)

Ribbing Pat: Knit 2, purl 2 Ribbing
Stockinette Stitch (St st): Knit sts on RS rows, purl sts on WS rows.
Cable Cuff: Work following the chart. Work the even-numbered rows as knit the k sts and purl the p sts. Over the center 9 Cable sts rep rnds 5–12.

Stripe Pat: Work 2 rnds each *bright white, light blue and medium blue; rep from *.

Gauge, Stockinette Stitch: 30 sts and 42 rows = 10 x 10 cm/4 x 4"

How to:
For the Right Sock with bright white, cast on 16 sts and for the Cable Cuff, follow the Stitch Chart in rows, working the increases as shown. At the end of the 19th row, cast on 40 sts. Divide sts over 4 needles (10 sts per needle) and join to work in rnds = 67 sts. Cont in Ribbing Pat until there are 32 rows/rnds from beg. For the turning ridge, purl 1 rnd, and over the Cable sts, work (p2tog) 3 times = 64 sts. Then turn work and cont in Ribbing Pat and Stripe Pat over all sts. After 30 rnds have been worked in Stripe Pat work 5 rnds in St st with bright white, and on the 1st rnd, fold the Cable Cuff to outside and work 1 cast-on st tog with corresponding st on needle. Cont with light blue in St st, dividing sts on the needles so that

the Cable Cuff is half on the 1st needle and half on the 2nd needle. Work the Heel Flap with reinforced Heel following the Basic Course on pages 26–27. After the Heel, work the Gusset decreases until there are 60 sts. When Foot measures 18 (19.5) cm/7 (7½)", work Star Toe following instructions on page 140.

Stitch Chart

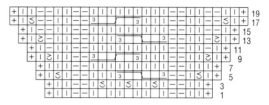

Stitch Key
+ = 1 selvage st   − = 1 purl st   I = 1 knit st   (blank) = no st
⊠ = M1 (knit into back loop of strand between 2 sts)
⊠ = M1-Purl (purl through back loop into strand between 2 sts)
= slip 3 sts to cn and hold to front of work, knit 3, then knit 3 from cn
= slip 3 sts to cn and hold to back of work, knit 3, then knit 3 from cn

---

Ribbed-Cabled Socks
Size: Adult 8/9 (9/10)

Materials:
Approx 100 g bright white, approx 50 g each light blue and medium blue (80% Wool, 20% Polyamide, Yardage = 210 m/50 g), 1 set (5) dpn size 2.5 mm (US 1), 1 Cable needle (cn)

Ribbing Pat: Knit 2, purl 2 Ribbing
Stockinette Stitch (St st): Knit sts on RS rows, purl sts on WS rows.
Cable: Work following the chart. Work rnds 1–10 once, then rep rnds 3–10.

Gauge, Stockinette Stitch: 30 sts and 42 rows = 10 x 10 cm/4 x 4"

How to:
With medium blue cast on 64 sts (= 1st needle 12 sts, 2nd needle 20 sts, 3rd and 4th needles 16 sts each) and for the cuff band work Ribbing Pat for 2 rnds with medium blue and 16 rnds with light blue, then for the turning ridge knit 1 rnd with light blue and cont in Ribbing Pat for 6 rnds. Change to bright white and work as follows: 12 sts Ribbing Pat, 6 sts Cable inc 3 sts on the 1st rnd following Stitch Chart 3 = 9 sts for Cable; 46 sts Ribbing Pat beg with purl 2. After 32 rnds above rib band cont in St st, and on the 1st rnd, dec 3 sts over the Cable and place the first 3 sts of the 2nd needle to the 1st needle and place the last st of the 2nd, 3rd and 4th needles to the following needle = 16 sts per needle. After 6 rnds, work the Heel Flap with reinforced Heel following the Basic Course on pages 26–27. After the Heel, cont in St st and work the Gusset decreases until there are 60 sts. When Foot measures 18 (19.5) cm/7 (7½)", work Star Toe following the instructions on page 140.

Finishing:
Fold Cuff band at turning ridge to outside.

Stitch Chart

Stitch Key
+ = 1 selvage st
− = 1 purl st
☐ = 1 knit st
⊠ = M1 (knit into back loop of strand between 2 sts)
= slip 3 sts to cn and hold to front of work, knit 3, then knit 3 from cn
 = slip 3 sts to cn and hold to back of work, knit 3, then knit 3 from cn

Medium Blue Cuffed Socks
Size: Adult 8/9 (9/10)

Materials:
Approx 100 g medium blue, approx 50 g each light blue and bright white (80% Wool, 20% Polyamide, Yardage = 210 m/50 g), 1 set (5) dpn size 2.5 mm (US 1), 1 Cable needle (cn)

Ribbing Pat: Knit 2, purl 2 Ribbing
Stockinette Stitch (St st): Knit sts on RS rows, purl sts on WS rows.
Cable over 17 sts: Work following the chart. Rep rows 1–8.
Gauge, Stockinette Stitch: 30 sts and 42 rows = 10 x 10 cm/4 x 4"

How to:
With bright white cast on 17 sts and work Cable for 128 rows. Join the sts on needle with the cast on sts to from a ring. Along the left side edge of the cable band, with light blue pick up 64 sts (1 st in every 2 rows) (= 16 sts per needle) and work 5 rnds in Ribbing Pat, then bind off sts. Along right side of cable band, with medium blue pick up 64 sts so that the beginning of rnd is at the cable band seam, and work in Ribbing Pat for 8 rnds. For the turning ridge, purl 1 rnd, then turn work and cont in Ribbing Pat for 28 rnds. Work 4 rnds in St st, then work the Heel Flap with reinforced Heel following the instructions on pages 26–27. After the Heel, cont in St st and work Gusset decreases until there are 60 sts. When Foot measures 18 (19.5) cm/7 (7½)" work Star Toe following the instructions on page 140.

Finishing:
Fold Cable band at turning ridge to outside.

Stitch Chart

Stitch Key
⊞ = 1 selvage st
⊟ = 1 purl st
☐ = 1 knit st
◌ = M1 (knit through back loop into strand between 2 sts)
= slip 3 sts to cn and hold to front of work, knit 3, knit 3 from cn.
= slip 3 sts to cn and hold to back of work, knit 3, knit 3 from cn.

Jeans Socks with Studs
Size: Adult 8/9 (9/10)

Materials:
Approx 100 g medium blue (80% Wool, 20% Polyamide, Yardage = 210 m/50 g), 1 set (5) dpn size 2.5 mm (US 1), Studs if desired.

Stockinette Stitch (St st): Knit sts on RS rows, purl sts on WS rows; in rnds, knit every rnd.

Gauge, Stockinette Stitch: 30 sts and 42 rows = 10 x 10 cm/4 x 4".

How to:
Cast on 60 sts over 4 needles (15 sts per needle) and work St st for 12 cm/4¾". Work the Heel Flap with reinforced Heel following the instructions on pages 26–27. When Foot measures 18.5 (19.5) cm/7 (7½)", work Star Toe following instructions on page 140.

Finishing:
The top of the cuff will roll approx 4 cm/1½" to the outside. Below the Rolled Edge, attach the studs in a zigzag line; see photo for placement. Before the zigzag, place a marker so that the end of the zigzag lines up with the beginning.

Socks with Rolled Edge
Size: Adult 8/9 (9/10)

Materials:
Approx 100 g blue and small amount white (80% Wool, 20% Polyamide, Yardage = 210 m/50 g), 2 sets (5) dpn size 2.5 mm (US 1), Studs if desired.

Stockinette Stitch (St st): Knit sts on RS rows, purl sts on WS rows; in rnds: knit every rnd.

Gauge in Stockinette Stitch: 30 sts and 42 rows = 10 x 10 cm/4 x 4".

How to:
With blue, cast on 60 sts over 4 needles (= 15 sts per needle) and for the 1st Rolled Edge work 20 rnds in St st, then place sts on hold. For 2nd edge, with white, cast on 60 sts and work same as 1st edge. Join the 2 edges as foll: Place the sts of the 1st edge parallel to the sts on the 2nd edge and with a 3rd needle, *work 1 st from first edge tog with 1 st on 2nd edge; rep from * until all sts are joined. Cont in St st with blue for 6 cm/2½". Work the Heel Flap with reinforced Heel following the instructions on pages 26–27. When Foot measures 18.5 (19.5) cm/7 (7½)", work Star Toe following the instructions on page 140.

Finishing:
Attach 7 studs (following manufacturer's instructions) to each of the rolled edges; see photo for placement.

Basic Course for:

The Boomerang Heel

The Boomerang Heel applies the principle of knitting with short rows. This heel sits particularly nicely on the foot.

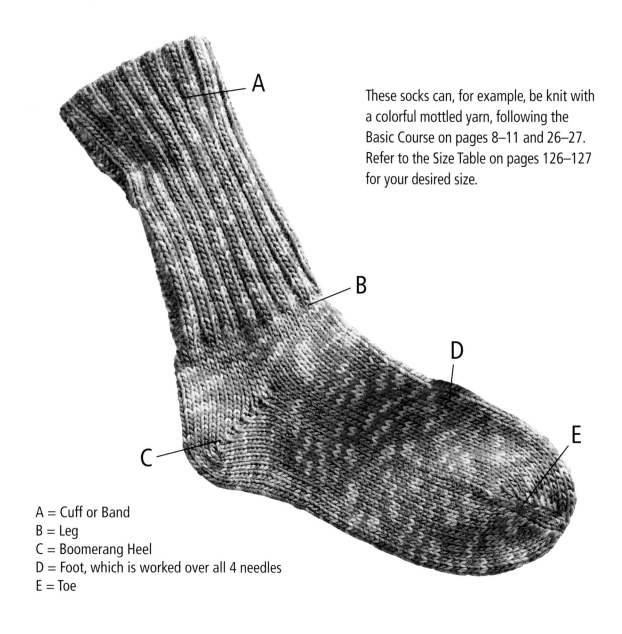

These socks can, for example, be knit with a colorful mottled yarn, following the Basic Course on pages 8–11 and 26–27. Refer to the Size Table on pages 126–127 for your desired size.

A = Cuff or Band
B = Leg
C = Boomerang Heel
D = Foot, which is worked over all 4 needles
E = Toe

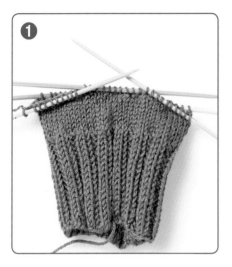

❶ The Boomerang Heel is worked over half of the stitches, that is, over the stitches of the 1st and 4th needles. The Heel stitches are divided into three parts.

❷ **The First Half Heel**: Row 1 (right side): Knit all stitches of the 1st needle, turn work. Row 2 (wrong side): Work a double selvage stitch as follows: bring yarn to front of work, slip next stitch purlwise, bring the yarn back to the front, pulling tightly, around the right needle creating an extra strand, or double stitch on the right needle (this will avoid a hole in the work).

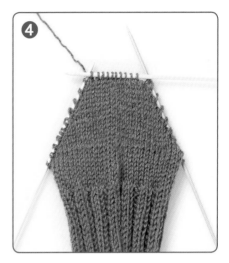

❸ After bringing the yarn back to the front, purl the remaining stitches of the 1st needle and all stitches of the 4th needle, turn work.

❹ Rep these 2 rows, until between the double stitches the number of stitches equals the middle third minus 2 stitches. Then knit rounds over all stitches of the 1st to the 4th needles, and on the 1st round, pick up each double stitch and knit it together with the corresponding stitch on the needle. Then work the 2nd Heel half.

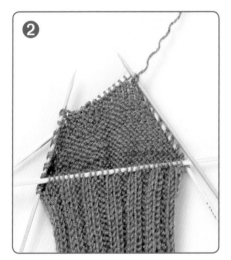

❺ **The 2nd Heel half**: Row 1 (right side): Knit the 1st and 2nd third of the stitches, turn work. Row 2 (wrong side): Work 1 double stitch, purl the remaining stitches of the middle third, turn work. Row 3: Work 1 double stitch, knit up to the double stitch, knit the double stitch together as before, knit the next stitch, turn work. Row 4: Work 1 double stitch, purl up to the double stitch, purl double stitch together as before, turn work.

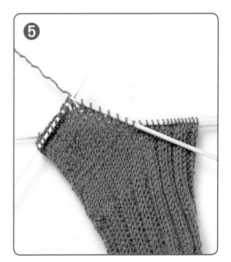

❻ Repeat rows 3 and 4 until all Heel stitches are worked. Then work all stitches of the sock and join to work in rounds to the desired foot length.

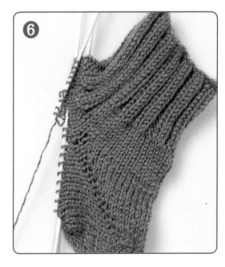

Pattern Hits
in Color Fever

Textured patterns give socks elasticity. This makes the fit even more comfortable, and the socks even more fun to knit. The colorful yarn also contributes to the knitting pleasure here.

Orange Socks
Size: Adult 8/9 (9/10)

Materials:
Approx 100 g orange color (75% Wool, 25% Polyamide, yardage = 210 m/50 g). 1 set (5) double-pointed needles (dpn) size 2.5mm (US 2) and one crochet hook size 2.5mm (US C/2)

Stockinette Stitch (St st): in rows, k on RS rows, p on WS rows; in rnds, k every rnd.
Cable and Rib Pat: over a multiple of 10 sts. Follow the chart. Rep rnds 1–4 three times and rnds 5–10 once, then rep rnd 11.

Gauge in Stockinette Stitch: 30 sts and 42 rows = 10 x 10 cm/4 x 4".

How to:
Cast on 60 sts and divide sts evenly over 4 needles (= 15 sts per needle). Join to work in rnds and work in Cable and Rib Pat for approx 4¾"/12 cm. Position the beg of rnd so that a knit rib is at the center back, then work the sts on needles 1 and 4 in St st and rem sts in Rib Pat, and cont for another 6 rnds. Work the boomerang heel with short rows as foll: place the sts of the 1st and 4th needles on one needle, leaving the sts on the 2nd and 3rd needles on hold, and work as foll: Row 1 (RS): Knit all sts, turn; Row 2 (WS): 1 double st (= with yarn in front of work, insert needle into 1st st purlwise. Slip the st to RH needle and bring yarn to back of work over the needle and pull tightly to make another st on RH needle), purl rem sts, turn; Row 3: 1 double st, k up to double st, turn; Row 4: 1 double st, purl up to double st, turn. Rep rows 3 and 4 until there are 8 sts in the center between the double sts, then work 2 rnds in pat over all 60 sts, and when working over the double st, k the st and extra strand on needle tog.

For the lower half of heel, work short rows as foll: Row 1 (RS): Knit 20, turn; Row 2 (WS): 1 double st, purl 9, turn; Row 3: 1 double st, knit up to double st, then knit double st and next st tog, turn; Row 4: 1 double st, purl up to double st, purl the double st and next st tog, turn. Rep rows 3 and 4 until all heel sts are worked. Then cont in rnds over all sts without gusset decs, working the sts on 1st and 4th needles in St st and on needles 2 and 3 in Rib Pat. Work even until piece measures 7½ (8)"/19 (20.5) cm from center of heel. Beg the toe shaping in St st following the basic instructions. Work the decs every 4th rnd once, every 3rd rnd twice, every 2nd rnd 3 times, then every rnd.

Finishing:
For each sock crochet 12 small rings as foll: for each ring, ch 4 and join with sl st in first ch to form a ring, ch 1 and work 12 sc in ring, then join rnd with sl st in beg ch-1. Sew the small rings to each other and sew to top edge of each sock, attaching one at each cable.

Stitch Key

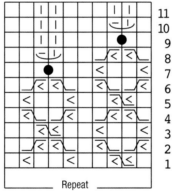

Repeat

$\boxed{|}$ = k1

$\boxed{<}$ = k1 through back lp (tbl)

$\boxed{}$ = p1

$\boxed{\subset|}$ = k1 and p 1 in 1 st

$\boxed{<<}$ = sl 1 st to cn and hold to front of work, k1 tbl, then k1 from cn

$\boxed{<}$ = sl 1 st to cn and hold to back of work, k1 tbl, then p1 from cn

$\boxed{<}$ = sl 1 st to cn and hold to front of work, p1, then k1 tbl from cn

● = 1 bobble: work 5 sts over 2 sts (= k2tog, yo, k same 2 sts tog, yo, k same 2 sts tog), turn, p5, turn, k5, turn, p5, turn, then k5tog

Patterned Socks
Size: Adult 8/9 (9/10)

Materials:

Approx 100 g in purple (75% Wool and 25% Polyamide, Yardage = approx 210 m/50 g), 1 set (5) dpn size 2.5 mm (US 1), 1 Cable needle (cn)

Stockinette Stitch (St st) in rnds: Knit every round.
Stockinette Stitch (St st) in rows: Knit sts on RS rows, purl sts on WS rows.
Band Pat: multiple of 10 sts. Follow the Stitch Chart A. Only the odd-numbered rnds are shown. Work the even-numbered rnds as knit the k sts and purl the p sts. Work the stitch repeat A (= rep-A) and work rnds 1–8 twice.
Diamond Pat: Work same as Band Pat following Stitch Chart A. Work the stitch repeat B (= rep-B). Work rnds 9–14 once, then rep rnds 15–42. On rnds 31 and 35, work the cable with the first 2 sts of the rnd and the last 2 sts of the previous rnd. The gray sections are worked in any of the patterns 1 to 7 given below, as desired.
Pattern 1: Rnd 1: *Knit 1, purl 1; rep from *. Rnd 2: *Purl 1, knit 1; rep from *. Rep rnds 1 and 2.
Pattern 2: *Purl 2 rnds, knit 2 rnds; rep from *.
Pattern 3: *Knit 1 through back loop, purl 1; rep from *.
Pattern 4: Odd rnds: *Yo, knit 2 tog through back loops; rep from *. Even rnds: Knit all sts.
Pattern 5: Work leaf following Stitch Chart B, working the even rnds as knit the k sts and yo's, purl the p sts.
Pattern 6: Rnds 1 and 2: *Knit 2, purl 2; rep from *. Rnds 3 and 4: *Purl 2, knit 2; rep from *.
Pattern 7: Knit the center 2 sts and purl the remaining and cross the center 2 sts every 2nd rnd (= knit the 2nd st in front of the 1st st, then knit the 1st st).

Gauge, Stockinette Stitch: 30 sts and 40 rows = 10 x 10 cm/4 x 4".
Gauge, in Diamond Pat: 35 sts = 10 cm/4".

How to:

Cast on 70 sts and divide sts evenly over 4 needles and join to work in rnds (= 1st needle 20 sts, 2nd and 3rd needles 17 sts each, 4th needle 16 sts). The beginning of rnd is the center back between 1st and 4th needles. For the cuff, work 16 rnds in Band Pat, then place the first 2 sts of the 1st needle to the 4th needle.

Cont with the Leg in Diamond Pat, working the center of the diamond cables in the desired pattern stitch. Work a total of 52 rnds in Diamond Pat, that is approx 10 cm/4" above band. On the last rnd, after the end of the 3rd needle, place the 34 sts of the 2nd and 3rd needles on hold. For the Boomerang heel place the sts of the 4th and 1st needles on one needle = 36 Heel sts, then work the Heel in Stockinette st following the Basic Course on pages 40–

41, on the 1st RS row, dec 6 stitches evenly across (preferably over the Cable Cross sts) = 30 Heel sts.

Then for the Foot cont in rnds over all 64 sts, place the 30 Heel sts for Sole in half on the 1st and 4th needle and divide the remaining 34 sts on the 2nd and 3rd needles. Cont the Sole sts in Stockinette Stitch and the sts on the 2nd and 3rd needles in Diamond Pat, orking the sts of the half diamond at the sides in Stockinette St and fill the full diamond in the desired pattern. Cont in pats as established until foot measures 19 (20.5) cm/7½ (8)".

Then work the Toe in Stockinette Stitch following the instructions on page 9, working 1 rnd knit, and dec 2 sts on each of the 2nd and 3rd needles = 60 sts. On the next rnd beg the toe decs, and rep decs every 4th rnd once, every 3rd rnd twice and every 2nd rnd 3 times, then every rnd until there are 8 sts. Cut yarn and draw through remaining sts.

Work the second Sock in same way, but fill the diamonds with different patterns.

Stitch Chart A

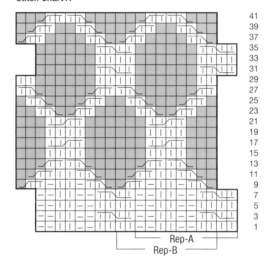

41
39
37
35
33
31
29
27
25
23
21
19
17
15
13
11
9
7
5
3
1

Rep-A
Rep-B

Stitch Chart B

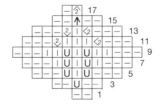

17
15
13
11
9
7
5
3
1

Stitch Key:

| $\vert$ = 1 knit st

| $-$ = 1 purl st

| U = 1 yarn over

| $\angle$ = knit 2 sts together

| $\angle$ = k2tog through back loops

| $\angle$ = purl 2 sts together

| $\uparrow$ = SK2P: sl 1 st knitwise, knit 2 sts together, pass the slipped st over k2tog

= slip 2 sts to cn and hold to front of work, knit 2, then knit 2 from cn

= slip 2 sts to cn and hold to back of work, knit 2, then knit 2 from cn

= slip 2 sts to cn and hold to front of work, work 1 st in pat, then k 2 from cn

= slip 1 st to cn and hold to back of work, knit 2, work 1 st from cn in pat

Cable Pattern Socks
Size: Adult 8/9 (9/10)

Materials:
Approx 100 g self-striping yarn in purple-red shades (75% Wool, 25% Polyamide, Yardage = 210 m/50 g), 1 set (5) double-pointed needles (dpn) size 3 mm (US 3) and 1 cable needle (cn)

Stockinette Stitch (St st): Knit sts on RS rows, purl sts on WS rows.
Cable Pat: multiple of 14 sts. Work following the chart. Work the stitch repeat and repeat rnds 1–4.
Brioche St: Rnd 1: slip 1 st purlwise with 1 yo, Rnd 2: Knit the st and the yo together. Rep rnds 1 and 2.

Gauge, Stockinette Stitch: 30 sts and 42 rows = 10 x 10 cm/4 x 4".

How to:
Cast on 56 sts over 4 needles (= 14 sts per needle) and in work Cable Pat for 16 cm/6¼". For the Heel work in St st over sts of the 1st and 4th needles, and on the 1st rnd inc 1 st on each of the 1st and 4th needles, and cont remaining sts as established. After another 4 rnds, work over the

30 Heel sts in the Boomerang Heel following the instructions on pages 40–41. After the Heel, cont over all sts in rnds without gusset decreases, working in St st over sts of 1st and 4th needles and cont Cable Pat over sts of 2nd and 3rd needles. After 19 (20.5) cm/7½ (8)" from heel center, work Toe following the Basic Course (see page 9), but work the first decrease only on the 1st and 4th needles, so that all needles have the same number of sts.

Stitch Chart

——— Repeat ———

Stitch Key:
☐ = 1 knit st   ⊟ = 1 purl st
⊽ = 1 Brioche st
= sl 1 st to cn and hold to back of work, knit 2, then purl 1 from cn

= slip 2 sts to cn and hold to front of work, purl 1, then knit 2 from cn

= slip 2 sts to cn and hold to front of work, knit 2, then knit 2 from cn

= slip 2 sts to cn and hold to back of work, knit 2, then knit 2 from cn

---

Socks with Colorful Gradients
Size: Adult 8/9 (9/10)

Materials:
Approx 100 g self-striping yarn in bright colors (75% Wool, 25% Polyamide, Yardage = 210 m/50 g), 1 set (5) double-pointed needles (dpn) size 3 mm (US 3) and Cable needle (cn)

Stockinette Stitch (St st): Knit sts on RS rows, purl sts on WS rows.

Brioche St: Rnd 1: slip 1 st purlwise with 1 yo, Rnd 2: Knit the st and the yo together. Rep rnds 1 and 2.
Cable Pat: multiple of 10 sts. Work following the chart. Only the odd-numbered rnds are shown. Work the even-numbered rnds as knit the k sts and purl the p sts or in pat as established. Work the stitch rep around. Work rnds 1–50 once, then rep rnds 1–12.

Gauge, Stockinette Stitch: 30 sts and 42 rows = 10 x 10 cm/4 x 4".

How to:
Cast on 60 sts over 4 needles (= 15 sts per needle) and work in Cable Pat for 60 rnds. For the Heel work in St st over sts of the 1st and 4th needle and cont over remaining sts in pat as established. Work 4 more rnds then work Boomerang Heel following the Basic Course on pages 40–41. After of the Heel work in rnds over all sts without gusset decreases, working the center 30 sts of the 2nd and 3rd needles in Cable Pat and cont the remaining sts in Stockinette St. After 19 (20.5) cm/7½ (8)" from heel center work the Toe following the Basic Course (see page 9).

Stitch Key:
☐ = 1 knit st   ⊟ = 1 purl st
⊽ = 1 Brioche st
= slip 1 st to cn and hold to back of work, knit 2, purl 1 from cn

Stitch Chart

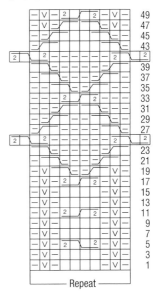

——— Repeat ———

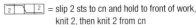
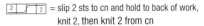

= slip 2 sts to cn and hold to front of work, purl 1, then knit 2 from cn

= slip 2 sts to cn and hold to front of work, knit 2, then knit 2 from cn

= slip 2 sts to cn and hold to back of work, knit 2, then knit 2 from cn

Socks in Exotic Colors and Patterns

SOCKS WITH TURKISH PATTERNS IN THE TREND COLOR LEMON

Bold colors and elaborate patterns take us into the world of the ancient Eastern empires.

A Tip:
For enchanting socks,
sew small sparkling stones, sequins, or
pendants to them. You'll find a wide
selection in stores.

Socks with Turkish Pattern
Size: Adult 9/10 (10/11) 11/12

Materials:
Approx 100 g each green mix and blue (75% Wool and 25% Polyamide, Yardage = approx 400 m/50 g), 1 set (5) dpn size 2.5 mm (US 1)

Main Pat: over 32 (34) 34 sts: Follow the Color Chart. Carry colors not in use loosely across WS. All sts and rows are shown. Rep rnds 1-17.

Border Pat: Multiple of 17 sts: Follow the Color Chart over the 17 sts and 9 rnds as outlined in black.

Sole Pat: *3 sts green, 3 sts blue; rep from *.

Band Pat: Multiple of 3 sts: Rnd 1: *knit 1, knit 1 but do not drop from left needle, bring yarn to front and purl it together with next st on needle; rep from *. Rnd 2: Knit all sts. Rep rnds 1 and 2.

Gauge, Stockinette Stitch: 28 sts and 40 rows = 10 x 10 cm/4 x 4"

How to:
For the Toe with dpn and green, cast on 6 sts and work Basic Course on pages 52–53 until there are 18 sts. Work in Stockinette St, working the 7 soles sts both sides of the center st in Sole Pat. For the extension, inc each side of 2 center sts (4 sts inc'd) every 2nd rnd 10 (11) 11 times, working increased sts into Sole Pat = 34 stitches. Over the center 15 stitches work the Instep and begin the Main Pat each side of the center sts and increase 3 stitches (= the 20 stitches between the two arrows on the chart). Work the increase stitches of the Foot into the pattern = 61 (65) 65 sts.

After 19 (20) 21 cm/7½ (8) 8½" from the Toe, work the Instep and Heel following the Basic Course, working the 4 increases (in St st) every 2nd round 7 (7) 8 times = 89 (93) 97 stitches.

Over the center 19 (21) 21 stitches, work the Sole stitches of the Cap in Stockinette st with blue. On both sides, knit the last or the first Cap st with one st from the side Sole sts together 13 (13) 15 times = 63 (67) 67 stitches.

Continue to work over all stitches in pats as established, and on the 1st round, follow the Basic Course and decrease 2 stitches = 61 (65) 65 stitches. After 2 rounds from beg of Leg, work all stitches in Main Pat, working the 17-stitch repeat 4 times and on the 1st round, increase 7 (3) 3 stitches evenly around = 68 stitches. When Leg measures 8 cm/3¼"—end with a pat rnd 17—work 2 rounds in green mix, 4 rounds in blue, 2 rounds in green mix and 6 rounds in blue. Then work 9 rounds in Border Pat, working the stitch repeat 4 times and reverse the colors (that is, the flowers in green mix and the background in blue). After 9 rnds of Border Pat have been worked, cont with blue only and work in Band Pat for 5 cm/2", and on the 1st round decrease 2 stitches = 66 stitches. Then bind off all stitches loosely.

Color Key

☐ = 1 st in blue

☐ = 1 st in green mix

Color Chart

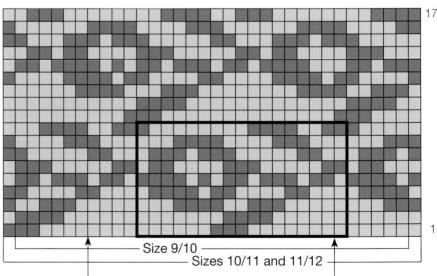

Socks with Rolled Edge
Size: Adult 8/9 (9/10)

Materials:
Approx 100 g red and a small amount orange (75% Wool and 25% Polyamide, Yardage = approx 210m/50 g), 1 set (5) dpn each sizes 2.5 and 3 mm (US 1 and 3), 12 star buttons

Stockinette Stitch (St st): Knit sts on RS rows, purl sts on WS rows.

Gauge, Stockinette Stitch: 30 sts and 42 rows = 10 x 10 cm/4 x 4" using size 2.5 mm (US 1) needles.

How to:
With size 2.5 mm (US 1) needles and red, cast on 60 stitches (= 15 stitches per needle) and for the 1st Rolled Edge work 16 rounds in Stockinette st. For the 2nd Rolled Edge, with 3 mm (US 3) dpn and orange, cast on 60 stitches and work 14 rounds

in Stockinette st. Then with red and 2.5 mm (US 1) needle, knit 1 stitch from each needle tog until all stitches are joined. Cont with 2.5 mm (US 1) needles and work in Stockinette st for 7 cm/2¾" from rolled edge. Work the Boomerang Heel following the Basic Course on pages 40 and 41. After the Heel, work in rnds over all sts without gusset decreases. After 17.5 (19) cm/7 (7½)" from heel center, work 4 rounds in orange, then work Toe in red following the Basic Course (see page 9). Cut yarn, draw through remaining stitches and secure.

Finishing
Sew six star buttons on each sock below the Rolled Edge.

Socks with Chain Ties
Size: Adult 8/9 (9/10)

Materials:
Approx 100 g self-striping in reds (75% Wool and 25% Polyamide, Yardage = approx 210m/50 g), 1 set (5) dpn size 2.5 mm (US 1), Swarovski crystal cut beads in various colors, wide elastic stretch yarn

Ribbing Pat: Knit 2, purl 2 Ribbing
Stockinette Stitch (St st): Knit sts on RS rows, purl sts on WS rows.

Gauge, Stockinette Stitch: 30 sts and 42 rows = 10 x 10 cm/4 x 4".

Note: To have matching socks, begin each sock at the same color section.

How to:
Cast on 60 stitches (= 15 stitches per needle) and work in Ribbing Pat for 6 rnds. Work eyelet rnd as

foll: *K2tog, yo twice; rep from * around. Knit next rnd and knit the double yo dropping the extra wrap. Cont in St st until 11 cm/4½" from beg.
Work the Boomerang Heel following the Basic Course on pages 40 and 41. After the Heel, work in rnds over all sts without gusset decreases. After 18.5 (22) cm/7¼ (8½)" from heel center, work Toe in Stockinette st following the Basic Course (see page 9). Cut yarn, draw through remaining stitches and secure.

Finishing
For each sock, make a chain tie as follows: String beads with the elastic stretch yarn and in desired colorway, for 16 cm/6¼", weave the yarn back through last 6 cm/2½" of beads and continue with the 2nd set and string beads for approx 10 cm/4". Weave the tie through the eyelet rnd, with the 6 cm/2½" section of beads hanging at the center outer edge and skipping 5 eyelet holes. Knot and secure the ends of the ties.

From the Toe up!

It begins with a few stitches at the tip of the toe—what a great technique! You can try on the sock at any time as you work, to determine the foot length that'll fit perfectly.

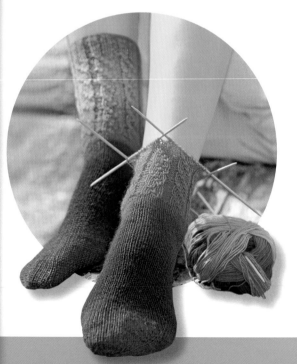

Yarn: : Design: Hug

51

The 4-Step Method
Socks knit from the toe up

MATERIALS:

• 1 set (5) double-pointed needles (dpn). You can find these needles in various lengths, from 10 cm/4", 15 cm/6" and 20 cm/8". The shorter needles are especially suitable for the first round, where there are just a few stitches on the needles. When there are more stitches on the needle, change to the longer needles.

• Yarn, i.e., sock yarn or wool yarn; see instructions for the individual patterns.

Step ① Toe

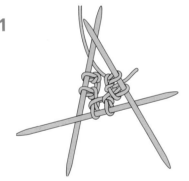

1. The cast on is the same for every type of sock. For the tip of the toe, cast on 6 sts and divide sts over 3 needles and join to work in rnds (ILL. 1). Make sure the lower edge of all sts faces inward and that no sts are twisted. Mark the end of the round with a stitch marker. You can also use a contrasting color yarn marker. Move the marker at the end of every rnd. It is an easy way to know when the round is complete.

Then knit 1 rnd. On the next rnd work a left-leaning increase in each st (ILL. 2). That is work 2 sts in 1 st as follows: insert the left needle from back to front into the underlying loop of the previous knit st and knit this loop.

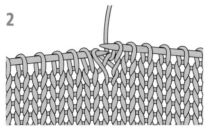

2. Continue in Stockinette Stitch over these 12 sts, and on the following 2nd rnd work left-leaning increase as before into every 2nd st = 18 sts. These sts are divided as follows: The 1st st of the rnd forms the right center st, the following 8 sts form the Instep, the following st forms the left center st and the remaining 8 sts form the sole. For the extension, increase each side of 2 center sts (4 sts inc'd) of the toe every 2nd rnd, working 1 right-leaning increase after the 2 center sts (ILL. 3). That is work 2 sts in 1 st as follows: insert the right needle from front to back into the underlying loop behind the following knit st and knit this loop. Then knit the st on the needle.

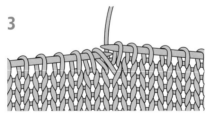

3. Then work 1 left-slanting dec before the 2 center st = 4 increases every rnd. Rep these increases every 2nd rnd until there are the designated number of sts on the Size Table on pages 142–143 or as the instructions state.

Step ② Foot, Heel, and Instep

Divide the sts over 4 needles as follows: Divide the sts from the right center st up to the left center st evenly over the 1st and 2nd needles—this forms the Instep. Divide the remaining sts evenly over the 3rd and 4th needle for the Sole. For the foot length work as many rnds or cm/in as designated on the Size Table or as stated in the instructions. Next, for the Instep in every 2nd rnd work 1 left-slanting increase to the right of the center st and 1 right-slanting increase to the left of the center st. Rep these increases until there are the number of sts designated on the Size Table or as stated in the instructions. At the same time, with the 3rd Instep increase, begin the increases for the Heel. For these increases, work 1 left-slanting increase to the left of the center st and 1 right-slanting increase to the right of the center st. Rep these increase until there are the number of sts designated on the Table or as stated in the instructions. The Instep and Heel end on the same round.

Step ③ Cap

For the Cap, work back and forth in rows over the center Sole sts on the 3rd and 4th needles; refer to the number of sts on the Size Table or in the instructions. On both sides of the Cap are the Heel sts. Work the sts of Instep on the 1st and 2nd needles as well as right side Heel sts and all Cap sts. Work SKP with the last Cap st and the 1st left side Heel st (ILL. 4). To do this, slip the 1st st knitwise and knit the following st. Then insert the left needle from left to right into the slipped st and pass it over the knit st and off the needle.

4

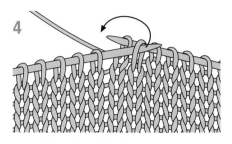

4. Turn the work and slip the 1st Cap st purlwise, with the yarn on front of work. Purl the remaining sts of the Cap, and purl the last st of the following right side Heel st together (ILL. 5). To do this, the yarn is at the front of the work as for working a purl st. Insert needle from right to left through both sts, purl the sts together and drop them from the left needle.

5

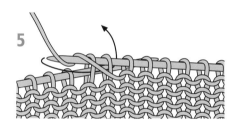

5. *Turn the work again and the slip the 1st st knitwise, with the yarn in back of work. Knit the Cap sts, and purl the last st with the following left side Heel st together.
Turn the work again and slip the 1st Cap st purlwise, with yarn in front of work. Purl the Cap sts, and purl the last st with the following right side Heel st together. Rep from * as many times as indicated on the Size Table or stated in the Instructions. Note: For larger socks, it may be that the sts of the Instep are knit into the Cap.

Step ④ Leg

The Leg begins with the end of the Cap. On the 1st rnd, work SKP with the last Cap st and the following st (ILL. 6). Now the yarn lies at the back of the work, as if to work a knit st. Insert the right needle from left to right into both sts, draw the yarn through and drop the sts from left needle.

6

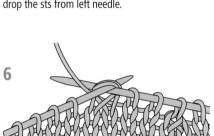

6. Thus, the original number of sts is reached. Work to the desired Leg length then bind off all sts loosely, in pattern.

Left Sock: For socks with a lateral pattern on the leg, after the Cap sts, work the Leg in reverse.

Step ①

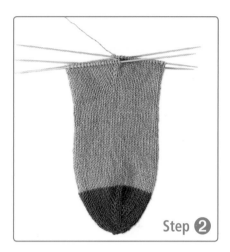
Step ②

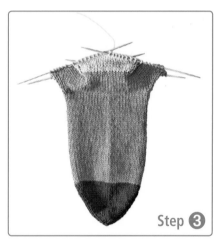
Step ③

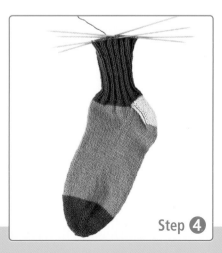
Step ④

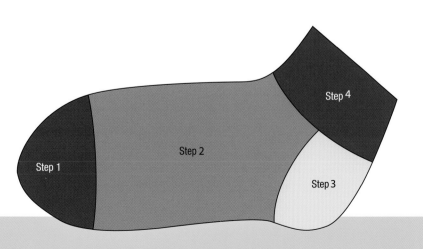
Step 1 / Step 2 / Step 3 / Step 4

Rainbow Socks
Size: Adult 8/9 (10/11)

Materials:
Approx 100 g sock yarn with colorful gradient (75% Wool, 25% Polyamide, Yardage = 210 m/50 g), 1 set (5) dpn size 2.5 mm (US 1), 1 Cable needle (cn)

Stockinette Stitch (St st) in rnds: Knit every rnd.
Stockinette Stitch in rows: Knit sts on RS rows, purl sts on WS rows.
Reverse Stockinette Stitch in rnds: Purl every rnd.
Cable Pat: multiple of 7 sts. Work following the chart. Only the odd-numbered rnds are shown. Work the even-numbered rnds as knit the k sts and purl the p sts. Work rnds 1–8 for 5 (6) times, then work rnds 9 and 10 for 5 times.

Gauge, Stockinette Stitch: 28 sts and 40 rows = 10 x 10 cm/4 x 4".

How to:
For the Toe with dpn cast on 6 sts and work Basic Instructions on pages 52–53 until there are 18 sts. Work in Stockinette St. For the extension, inc each side of 2 center sts (4 sts inc'd) every 2nd rnd 9 (11) times = 54 (62) sts. Cont in Stockinette Stitch for 16.5 (19) cm/6½ (7½)" from Toe. For the Instep inc 1 st at each side of the center st every 2nd rnd 8 (9) times. And with the 3rd Instep increase, work the increase for the Heel every 2nd row 6 (7) times = 82 (94) sts. Then over the center 16 (20) sts of the Sole work the Cap in St st. On both sides, knit the last or the first Cap st with one st from the side Sole sts together 12 (14) times = 58 (66) sts. Then for the Leg work 3 rnds

Stockinette Stitch over all sts, and on the 1st rnd work SKP with the last Cap st and the following st and work knit 2 tog with the first Cap st and the previous st. For the larger size work 1 more decrease to keep to the Pattern st = 56 (63) sts. Then cont in Cable Pat for 12.5 cm/5" = 50 rnds (14.5 cm/5¾" = 58 rnds). Bind off all sts loosely in pat.

Stitch Chart

–	I	I	–	I	I	–	9
–	I	I	I	⟋T	I	–	7
–	I	I	I	⟋T	I	–	5
–	I	I	I	⟋T	I	–	3
–	I	⟋T	I	I	I	–	1

Stitch Key

I = 1 knit st

– = 1 purl st

⟋T = Cross 2 Right:
slip 1 st to cn and hold to back of work, knit 1, knit 1 from cn

---

With Fringe Yarn in Wave Pattern
Size: Adult 10

Materials:
Approx 100 g sock yarn each in orange, yellow and white (75% Wool, 25% Polyamide, Yardage = 210 m/50 g), approx 50 g fringe yarn each in orange, yellow and white 1 set (5) double-pointed needles (dpn) size 2.5 mm (US 1)

Stockinette Stitch (St st) in rnds: knit every rnd.
Wave Pat: Multiple of 16 sts. Work following the Stitch Chart. Rep rnds 1 and 2.
Stripe Pat A in Wave Pat with sock yarn: *2 rnds each in white and yellow, 6 rnds in white, 2 rnds each in orange and yellow, 6 rnds in orange; rep from *.
Stripe Pat B in Wave Pat: *1 rnd double strand in orange fringe yarn, 1 rnd in orange sock yarn, 1 rnd double strand in yellow fringe yarn, 1 rnd in yellow sock yarn, 6 rnds in orange sock yarn, 1 rnd double strand in white fringe yarn, 1 rnd in white sock yarn, 1 rnd double strand in yellow fringe yarn, 6 rnds in white sock yarn; rep from *.

Gauge, Stockinette Stitch with sock yarn: 28 sts and 40 rows = 10 x 10 cm/4 x 4".

How to:
For the Toe with dpn and orange sock yarn cast on 6 sts and work Basic Course on pages 52–53 until there are 18 sts. Cont in Stockinette St. For the extension, inc each side

of 2 center sts (4 sts inc'd) every 2nd rnd 11 times = 62 sts. On the next rnd work Stripe Pat A over the Instep and St st over the Sole sts and inc 1 st on each Sole needle = 64 sts. Work Stripe Pat A for 14 cm/5½" = 46 rnds working Instepincrease every 2nd row 8 times. And with the 3rd Instep increase, work the increase for the Heel every 2nd row 6 times = 92 sts. Then over the center 18 sts of the Sole, work the Cap in Stockinette St. On both sides, knit the last or the first Cap st with one st from the side Sole sts together 13 times = 66 sts. Then for the Leg work Stripe Pat over all sts, and on the 1st rnd, work SKP with the last Cap st and the following st and work k2tog with the first Cap st and the previous st = 64 sts. After 70 rnds have been worked in Stripe Pat A (not counting the Cap), work 60 rnds in Stripe Pat B. Change to white sock yarn and knit 1 rnd, purl 1 rnd, knit 1 rnd, then bind off all sts knitwise.

Stitch Chart

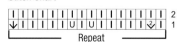

Repeat

Stitch Key

⤵ = k2tog

I = 1 knit st

U = 1 yo

⤵ = SKP: slip 1 st knitwise, knit 1 st and pass the slipped st over knit 1

Socks with Overlay
Size: Adult 9/10 (10/11)

Materials:
100 g orange (75% Wool, 25% Polyamide, Yardage = 210 m/50 g), 50 g pastel mix (61% Polyamide, 39% Wool, Yardage = 125 m/50 g), 1 set (5) dpn size 2.5 mm (US 1)

Stockinette Stitch (St st) in rnds: Knit every rnd.
Stockinette Stitch in rows: Knit sts on RS rows, purl sts on WS rows.
Reverse Stockinette Stitch in rnds: Purl every rnd.
Ribbing Pat A: multiple of 6 sts + 1: *1 st Reverse Stockinette St, 5 sts Stockinette St; rep from *, end with 1 st Reverse Stockinette St.
Ribbing Pat B: multiple of 3. *2 sts Stockinette St, 1 st Reverse Stockinette St; rep from *.

Gauge, Stockinette Stitch with orange: 28 sts and 40 rows = 10 x 10 cm/4 x 4".

How to:
For the Toe, with dpn and orange, cast on 6 sts and work Basic Course on pages 52–53 until there are 18 sts. Work in St st. For the extension, inc each side of 2 center sts (4 sts inc'd) every 2nd rnd 10 times = 58 sts. Then work in pats as follows: knit the center st and the following 2 sts, work Ribbing Pat A over following 24 sts, inc 1 st (= 25

sts for multiple of 6 + 1), and knit remaining sts = 59 sts. After 18 (19) cm/7 (7½)" from beg, for the Instep inc 1 st (in St st) at each side of the center st every 2nd rnd 8 (9) times. And with the 3rd Instep increase, work the increase for the Heel every 2nd row 6 (7) times = 87 (91) sts. Then over the center 18 (20) sts of the Sole, work the Cap in St st. On both sides, knit the last or the first Cap st with one st from the side Sole sts together 14 (16) times = 59 sts. Then for the Leg work in Ribbing Pat B over all sts, and on the 1st rnd work SKP with the last Cap st and the following st and work knit 2 tog with the first Cap st and the previous st = 57 sts. Be careful that the purl st of the Instep lines up with the p st in Ribbing Pat B. When total Leg length measures 16 cm/6¼", bind off all sts loosely in pat.

Overlay (make 2): With pastel mix, cast on 51 sts over 4 needles, join and work in rnds in Ribbing Pat B for 10 cm/4", then bind off all sts in pat. Pull the overlay over the Leg.

Slippers for Everyone
Size: Child 7½/8 (Adult 7/8) Adult 10/11

Materials:
100 (100) 150 g colorful self-striping yarn (80% Acrylic, 20% Wool, Yardage = 90 m/50 g), 1 set (5) dpn size 6 mm (US 10)

Stockinette Stitch (St st) in rnds: Knit every rnd.
Stockinette Stitch in rows: Knit sts on RS rows, purl sts on WS rows.
Reverse Stockinette Stitch in rnds: Purl every rnd.
Reverse Stockinette Stitch in rows: Purl sts on RS rows, knit sts on WS rows.

Gauge, Stockinette Stitch: 10 sts and 16 rows = 10 x 10 cm/4 x 4".

How to:
For the Toe with dpn and desired color, cast on 6 sts and work the Basic Course on pages 52–53 until there are 18 sts. Work in Stockinette St. For the extension, inc each side of 2 center sts (4 sts inc'd) every 2nd rnd 1 (2) 3 times = 22 (26) 30 sts. After 13 (16.5) 19.5 cm /5 (6½) 7½" from beg, for the Instep inc 1 st at each side of the

center st every 2nd rnd 3 (4) 5 times. And with the 3rd Instep increase, work the increase for the Heel every 2nd row 1 (2) 3 times = 30 (38) 46 sts. Then over the center 6 (8) 10 sts of the Sole sts work the Cap in St st. On both sides, knit the last or the first Cap st with one st from the side Sole sts together 4 (6) 8 times = 22 (26) 30 sts. Then for the Leg work 2 rnds in St st over all sts, and on the 1st rnd work SKP with the last Cap st and the following st and work knit 2 tog with the first Cap st and the previous st = 20 (24) 28 sts. Work 3 (4) 5 rnds more. Divide the work in the center of the Instep and for the Flap, work back and forth in rows in Reverse Stockinette Stitch and inc 1 st each end of every 2nd row twice = 24 (28) 32 sts. After 7 rows of Reverse Stockinette St, bind off all sts loosely purlwise on WS.

The Lodge Look

Lodge Inspiration

Take a vacation from everyday life! With sneaker socks or long socks you can make your feet feel good.

Socks with Straps
Size: Adult 7/8 (9/10) 10/11

Materials:
Approx 100 g brown (75% Wool, 25% Polyamide, Yardage = 210 m/50 g), 50 g or small amount black (75% Wool, 25% Polyamide, Yardage = 210 m/50 g), 1 set (5) dpn size 2.5 mm (US 1)
2 belt buckles 3 x 2 cm/1¼ x ¾"

Stockinette Stitch (St st) in rnds: Knit every rnd.
Stockinette Stitch in rows: Knit sts on RS rows, purl sts on WS rows.

Gauge, Stockinette Stitch: 28 sts and 40 rows = 10 x 10 cm/4 x 4".

How to:
For the Toe, with dpn and brown, cast on 6 sts and work Basic Course on pages 52–53 until there are 18 sts. Work in Stockinette St. For the extension, inc each side of 2 center sts (4 sts inc'd) every 2nd rnd 9 (10) 11 times = 54 (58) 62 sts. Then cont in Stockinette Stitch until 16 (18) 19 cm/6¼ (8) 7½" above Toe. For the Instep, inc 1 st at each side of the center st every 2nd rnd 7 (8) 9 times. And with the 3rd Instep increase, work the increase for the Heel every 2nd row 5 (6) 7 times = 78 (86) 94 sts. Then over the center 16 (18) 20 sts of the Sole, work the Cap in St st. On both sides, knit the last or the first Cap st with one st from the side Sole sts together 10 (12) 14 times = 58 (62) 66 sts. Then for the Leg work in Stockinette Stitch over all sts, and on the 1st rnd work SKP with the last Cap st and the following st and work knit 2 tog with the first Cap st and the previous st = 56 (60) 64 sts. When leg measures 6.5 (7) 7.5 cm/2½ (2¾) 3", purl 1 rnd, then bind off all sts loosely.

Finishing:
For the Straps in black with dpn, cast on 10 sts. Divide sts over 3 needles and join to work in rnds. Work in Stockinette st for 22 (24) 26 cm/8½ (9½) 10¼" from beg. Bind off all sts. Sew open ends of tube together. Sew buckle to one edge. Place strap around top of Leg and weave the other end through the buckle.

Sport Sneaker Socks
Size: Adult 7/8 (9/10) 10/11

Materials:
Approx 50 g each green, white and red (75% Wool, 25% Polyamide, Yardage = 210m/50 g), 1 set (5) dpn size 2.5 mm (US 1)

Stockinette Stitch (St st) in rnds: Knit every rnd.
Stockinette Stitch in rows: Knit sts on RS rows, purl sts on WS rows.
Reverse Stockinette Stitch in rnds: Purl every rnd.
Reverse Stockinette Stitch in rows: Purl sts on RS rows, knit sts on WS rows.
Ribbing Pat: *1 st in Stockinette St, 1 st in Reverse Stockinette St; rep from *.
Stripe Pat: Worked in Stockinette St, *3 rnds white, 3 rnds green; rep from *.

Gauge, Stockinette Stitch: 28 sts and 40 rows = 10 x 10 cm/4 x 4".

How to:
For the Toe, with dpn and green, cast on 6 sts and work Basic Course on pages 52–53 until there are 18 sts. Work in Stockinette St. For the extension, inc each side of 2 center sts (4 sts inc'd) every 2nd rnd 9 (10) 11 times = 54 (58) 62 sts. Then knit 1 rnd with red. Cont in Stockinette St, working 21 (25) 29 rnds with green and 15 rnds in Stripe Pat, then cont with green. At the same time, after 16 (18) 19 cm/6¼ (7) 7½" above Toe, for the Instep inc 1 st at each side of the center st every 2nd rnd 7 (8) 9 times. And with the 3rd Instep increase, work the increase for the Heel every 2nd row 5 (6) 7 times = 78 (86) 94 sts. Then knit 1 rnd with red. Then over the center 16 (18) 20 sts of the Sole, work the Cap in St st with green. On both sides, knit the last or the first Cap st with one st from the side Sole sts together 10 (12) 14 times = 58 (62) 66 sts. Then for the Leg, work in Stockinette Stitch over all sts for 2 rnds, and on the 1st rnd work SKP with the last Cap st and the following st and work knit 2 tog with the first Cap st and the previous st = 56 (60) 64 sts. Then with white, knit 1 rnd and work 4 rnds in Ribbing Pat. Then place the center 14 Heel sts on hold and bind off the remaining sts. Over these 14 sts for the back flap work in short rows in Stockinette Stitch as follows: at end of every row leave 2 sts unworked and with 1 yo turn work, until 2 sts are left in center. Turn and work to end of row, working the extra yo at each turn together with corresponding st on needle. Turn and work to end of the following row, working yo's tog with sts as before. Beginning with a RS row, work long rows as follows: knit 8 sts, turn, purl 2, turn, knit 4, turn, cont in this way, working 2 more sts at end of every row, until all sts have been worked. On the last WS row, bind off 14 sts. Fold flap in half to WS and sew in place.

Socks with Fringe Yarn
Size: Adult 8/9 (10/11)

Materials:
100 g beige mix (45% Viscose, 40% Wool, 15% Polyamide, Yardage = 200 m/50 g, 50 g fringe yarn in beige (100% Polyester, Yardage = 100 m/50 g), 1 set (5) dpn size 2.5 mm (US 1)

Stockinette Stitch (St st) in rnds: Knit every rnd.
Stockinette Stitch in rows: Knit sts on RS rows, purl sts on WS rows.
Reverse Stockinette Stitch in rnds: Purl every rnd.
Square Pat: multiple of 8 sts. Work following the chart. All the rnds are shown. Work the stitch repeat around. Rep rnds 1 – 8, end with rnds 9 and 10. The letters at the side of the chart represent the color.
Ribbing Pat: *1 st in Stockinette St, 1 st in Reverse Stockinette St; rep from *.

Gauge, Stockinette Stitch: 28 sts and 40 rows = 10 x 10 cm/4 x 4".

How to:
For the Toe, with beige mix and dpn, cast on 6 sts and work Basic Course on pages 52–53 until there are 18 sts. Work in Stockinette Stitch For the extension, inc each side of 2 center sts (4 sts inc'd) every 2nd rnd 9 (11) times = 54 (62) sts. Cont in Stockinette Stitch until 16 (19) cm/6¼ (7½)" above Toe. For the Instep inc 1 st at each side of the center st every 2nd rnd 7 (9) times. And with the 3rd Instep increase, work the increase for the Heel every 2nd row 5 (7) times = 78 (94) sts. Then over the center 16 (20) sts of the Sole sts work the Cap in St st. On both sides, knit the last or the first Cap st with one st from the side Sole sts together 10 (14) times = 58 (66) sts. Then for the Leg work in Stockinette Stitch over all sts for 2 rnds, and on the 1st rnd work SKP with the last Cap st and the following st and work knit 2 tog with the first Cap st and the previous st = 56 (64) sts. Then work 50 (58) rnds in Square Pat. With beige mix knit 1 rnd, then work in Ribbing Pat for 3 cm/1¼". Bind off all sts loosely in pat.

Stitch Chart

I	I	I	I	I	I	I	I	10	B
I	I	I	I	I	I	I	I	9	B
I	–	I	–	/	–	I	–	8	A
I	–	I	–	/	–	I	–	7	A
I	–	I	–	/	–	I	–	6	A
I	–	I	–	/	–	I	–	5	A
I	–	I	–	/	–	I	–	4	A
I	–	I	–	/	–	I	–	3	A
I	I	I	I	I	I	I	I	2	B
I	I	I	I	I	I	I	I	1	B

Stitch Key
I = 1 knit st
– = 1 purl st
/ = slip 1 st knitwise, with yarn in back of work

A = beige mix
B = fringe yarn

For Little Feet

These designs make it a pleasure to knit socks for your little ones. And they are the perfect gift for the new little arrival.

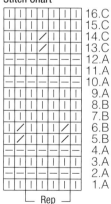

Kids' Socks with Buttons
Size: Child 6/6½ (7½/8)

Materials:
100 g each multicolor and white (45% Viscose, 40% Wool, 15% Polyamide, Yardage = 200 m/50 g), 2 buttons, 1 set (5) dpn size 2.5 mm (US 1)

Stockinette Stitch (St st) in rnds: Knit every rnd.
Stockinette Stitch in rows: Knit sts on RS rows, purl sts on WS rows.

Reverse Stockinette Stitch in rnds: Purl every rnd.
Stripe Pat A in Stockinette Stitch: *6 (8) rnds multicolor, 2 rnds white; rep from *.
Stripe Pat B: *4 rnds Stockinette Stitch in white, 1 rnd Stockinette Stitch in multicolor, 5 rnds Reverse Stockinette Stitch in multicolor; rep from * twice more = 30 rnds.
Ribbing Pat: *1 st in Stockinette St, 1 st in Reverse Stockinette St; rep from *.

Gauge, Stockinette Stitch: 28 sts and 40 rows = 10 x 10 cm/4 x 4".

How to:
For the Toe, with dpn and white, cast on 6 sts and work Basic Course on pages 52–53 until there are 18 sts. Work in St st. For the extension, inc each side of 2 center sts (4 sts inc'd) every 2nd rnd 7 (8) times = 46 (50) sts. Then cont in Stripe Pat A for 24 (30) rnds. Cont in Stockinette Stitch and multicolor. After 9 (12.5) cm/3½ (5)" from beg, for the Instep inc 1 st at each side of the center st every 2nd rnd 5 (6) times. And with the 3rd Instep increase, work the increase for the Heel every 2nd row 3 (4) times = 62 (70) sts. Then over the center 12 (14) sts of the Sole sts work the Cap in Stockinette Stitch with white. On both sides, knit the last or the first Cap st with one st from the side Sole sts together 7 (9) times = 48 (52) sts. Then for the Leg work in St st and multicolor over all sts, and on the 1st rnd work SKP with the last Cap st and the following st and work knit 2 tog with the first Cap st and the previous st = 46 (50) sts. After 6 (10) rnds Stockinette St, cont in Stripe Pat B for 30 rnds. For the Cuff, change to white and knit 1 rnd, then work 7 cm/2¾" in Ribbing Pat. Bind off sts up to the outer 11 sts and cont to work back and forth in rows in Ribbing Pat over these 11 sts for the Flap for 3.5 cm/1½". For the point, dec 1 st each end every 2nd row 3 times as follows: on a RS row, k1, SKP (= slip 1 st, knit 1, pass slipped st over knit 1), knit to last 3 sts, knit 2 together, knit 1. After all decreases there are 5 sts. Work next RS row as follows: Knit 2, slip 1 st, knit 2 sts together, pass slipped st over k2tog, knit 1. Cut yarn and draw through the remaining 3 sts and secure end.

Finishing:
Sew button to Flap and sock (see photo).

Kids' Socks with Stripes
Size: Child 6/6½ (7½/8)

Materials:
100 g each multicolor, white and orange (45% Viscose, 40% Wool, 15% Polyamide, Yardage = 200 m/50 g), 1 set (5) dpn size 2.5 mm (US 1)

Stockinette Stitch (St st) in rnds: Knit every rnd.
Stockinette Stitch in rows: Knit sts on RS rows, purl sts on WS rows.
Reverse Stockinette Stitch in rnds: Purl every rnd.
Stripe Pat: *4 rnds multicolor, 4 rnds orange, 4 rnds multicolor, 4 rnds white; rep from *.
Woven Pat A: multiple of 4 sts + 3. Work following the Stitch Chart. Every round is shown. Begin with the sts before the stitch rep, work the stitch rep, end with the sts after the rep. Rep rnds 1–16. The letters at the side represent the color used.

Woven Pat B: multiple of 4 sts. Work same as Pat A, but only work the sts between the stitch rep and rep rnds 1–16.
Ribbing Pat: *3 sts in Stockinette St, 2 sts in Reverse Stockinette St; rep from *.

Gauge, Stockinette Stitch: 28 sts and 40 rows = 10 x 10 cm/4 x 4".

How to:
For the Toe with multicolor and dpn, cast on 6 sts and work Basic Course on pages 52–53 until there are 18 sts. Work in Stockinette St. For the extension, inc each side of 2 center sts (4 sts inc'd) every 2nd rnd 7 (8) times = 46 (50) sts. Cont in pats as follows: right center st + 0 (1) st in Stockinette Stitch and Stripe Pat, work in Woven Pat A over the next 22 sts, and on the 1st rnd inc 1 st (for a multiple of 4 sts + 3) = 23 sts Woven Pat A, work remaining sts in Stockinette Stitch and Stripe Pat = 47 (51) sts. After 9.5 (12.5) cm/3¾ (5)" from beg, for the Instep inc 1 st at each side of the center st every 2nd rnd 5 (6) times. And with the 3rd Instep increase, work the increase for the Heel every 2nd row 3 (4) times = 63 (71) sts. Then over the center 12 (14) sts of the Sole, work the Cap in Stockinette Stitch and multicolor. On both sides, knit the last or the first Cap st with one st from the side Sole sts together 6 (8) times = 51 (55) sts. Then for the Leg over all Stockinette Stitch sts work in Woven Pat B, and on the 1st rnd work SKP with the last Cap st and the following st and work knit 2 tog with the first Cap st and the previous st = 48 (52) sts. After 36 (44) rnds have been worked in Woven Pat B, for the Cuff, work in Ribbing Pat with multicolor for 3 cm/1¼", and on the 1st rnd, increase 2 (3) sts = 50 (55) sts. Then bind off all sts loosely in pat.

Stitch Chart

											16.C

Stitch Key
- ☐ = 1 knit st
- ⊟ = Purl 1
- ⧄ = slip 1 knit st knitwise, with yarn in back of work

Rows: 16.C, 15.C, 14.C, 13.C, 12.A, 11.A, 10.A, 9.A, 8.B, 7.B, 6.B, 5.B, 4.A, 3.A, 2.A, 1.A

Rep

A = multicolor
B = orange
C = white

Striped Socks in Brioche Pattern
Size: Child 6/6½ (7½/8)

Materials:
100 g each lilac and pink (75% Wool, 25% Polyamide, Yardage = 210 m/50 g), 1 set (5) dpn size 2.5 mm (US 1)

Stockinette Stitch (St st) in rnds: Knit every rnd.
Stockinette Stitch in rows: Knit sts on RS rows, purl sts on WS rows.
Reverse Stockinette Stitch in rnds: Purl every rnd.
Ribbing Pat: *1 st in Stockinette St, 1 st in Reverse Stockinette St; rep from *.
Brioche Pat: multiple of 4 sts + 1: Work following the chart. Both rnds are shown. Work the stitch repeat around, end with working the 1st st once more. Rep rnds 1 and 2.
Stripe Pat in Brioche Pat: *3 rnds pink, 4 rnds lilac, 1 rnd pink, 4 rnds lilac, 2 rnds pink, 4 rnds lilac; rep from *.

Gauge, Stockinette Stitch: 28 sts and 40 rows = 10 x 10 cm/4 x 4".

How to:
For the Toe, with dpn and lilac, cast on 6 sts and work Basic Course on pages 52–53 until there are 18 sts. Work in Stockinette St. For the extension, inc each side of 2 center sts (4 sts inc'd) every 2nd rnd 6 (8) times = 42 (50) sts. Then work in pats as follows: Knit the right center st, work in Brioche st over the following 20 (24) sts, increasing 1 st (for a multiple of 4 sts + 1), knit remaining sts = 43 (51) sts. After 9 (12.5) cm/3½ (5)" from beg, for the Instep inc 1 st at each side of the center st every 2nd rnd 5 (6) times. And with the 3rd Instep increase, work the increase for the Heel every 2nd row 3 (4) times = 59 (71) sts. Then over the center 12 (14) sts of the Sole sts work the Cap in Stockinette Stitch with lilac. On both sides, knit the last or the first Cap st with one st from the side Sole sts together 6 (8) times = 47 (55) sts. Then for the Leg cont in Brioche st over all sts, and on the 1st rnd work SKP with the last Cap st and the following st and work knit 2 tog with the first Cap st and the previous st and dec 1 st over the Pat sts (for a multiple of 4 sts - work the 4-st rep around) = 44 (52) sts. When Leg measures 6.5 (9) cm/2½ (3½)" for the Cuff, work in Ribbing Pat for 10 cm/4", then bind off all sts loosely in pat.

Stitch Chart

—	■	—	●	—
—	—	○	—	○

2
1

Rep

Stitch Key
○ = slip the stitch purlwise with 1 yo
● = knit the stitch together with the yo
■ = knit the stitch together with the yo
— = 1 purl stitch

Baby Socks
Size: Child 4/5 (5/6) 6/6½)

Materials:
Approx 50 g each white mix, pink and yellow (65% Polyamide, 35% Wool, Yardage = 125 m/50 g), 1 set (5) dpn size 3 mm (US 3), 1 crochet hook size 3 mm (US D/3)

Stockinette Stitch in rnds: Knit every rnd.
Stockinette Stitch in rows: Knit sts on RS rows, purl sts on WS rows.
Stripe Pat: *1 rnd contrast color (CC), 2 rnds main color (MC); rep from *.

Gauge, Stockinette Stitch: 22 sts and 35 rows = 10 x 10 cm/4 x 4".

Version A: CC = white mix, MC = yellow
Version B: CC = white mix, MC = pink
Version C: CC = pink, MC = white mix

How to:
For the Toe, with dpn and MC, cast on 6 sts and work Basic Course on pages 52–53 until there are 18 sts. Work in Stockinette St. For the extension, inc each side of 2 center sts (4 sts inc'd) every 2nd rnd 2 (3) 4 times. Then on the following rnd, increase 2 sts = 28 (32) 36 sts. Then cont in Stripe Pat. After 7 (8) 9.5 cm/2¾ (3¼) 3¾" from beg, for the Instep inc 1 st at each side of the center st every 2nd rnd 4 (4) 5 times. And with the 3rd Instep increase, work the increase for the Heel every 2nd row 2 (2) 3 times = 40 (44) 52 sts. Then over the center 8 (8) 10 sts of the Sole sts work the Cap in St st with the MC. On both sides, knit the last or the first Cap st with one st from the side Sole sts together 5 (5) 7 times = 30 (34) 38 sts. Then for the Leg cont in Stripe Pat over all sts, and on the 1st rnd work SKP with the last Cap st and the following st and work knit 2 tog with the first Cap st and the previous st = 28 (32) 36 sts. After 7 (10) 13 rnds, for the Cuff facing, with MC, work 5 rnds Stockinette St, purl 1 rnd and 4 rnds Stockinette St. Then bind off all sts. Fold Cuff in half to inside at purl rnd and sew in place. With crochet hook, make a chain approx 50 (52) 54 cm/19½ (20½) 21" long and weave through the Cuff facing, beginning and ending at the center front.

Sock Quartet
at the Top of the Class

Light and airy

These short style socks—called sneaker socks—are the perfect footwear for summer. The airy lace pattern at the cuffs and at the top of the foot is best suited for warm weather.

There are no limits
to the choice of
color and pattern
combinations.
Let yourself be
inspired, grab
your yarn and
needles, and knit
your favorite socks.

Heel, Sole and Toe are knit
in Stockinette stitch in order
to fit smoothly in the shoe.
The Leg, which is always
seen, is often worked in a
pattern stitch. Small texture
patterns, bobbles, and cables can make nice accents,
as shown here.

Summer Socks
Size: Adult 9/10 (10/11)

Materials:
Approx 50 g each yellow, salmon and mint (55% Merino Wool, 20% Silk, 5% Polyamide, Yardage = 200 m/50 g), 1 set (5) dpn size 2.5 mm (US 1)

Stockinette Stitch (St st) in rnds: Knit every rnd.

Stockinette Stitch in rows: Knit sts on RS rows, purl sts on WS rows.

Reverse Stockinette Stitch in rnds: Purl every rnd.

Openwork Pat (over 25 sts): Follow Stitch Chart 1. Only the odd-numbered rnds are shown. Work the even-numbered rnds as knit the k sts and purl the p sts. Rep rnds 1–20.

Border Pat: Begins with a multiple of 8 sts. Follow Stitch Chart 2. **Note:** All the rnds are shown. Rep rnds 1–7.

Ribbing Pat: *1 st in Stockinette St, 1 st in Reverse Stockinette St; rep from *.

Stripe Pat: 2 rnds each salmon, yellow and mint

Gauge, Stockinette Stitch: 28 sts and 40 rows = 10 x 10 cm/4 x 4".

How to:
For the Toe, with dpn and yellow, cast on 6 sts and work Basic Course on pages 52–53 until there are 18 sts. Work in Stockinette St. For the extension, inc each side of 2 center sts (4 sts inc'd) every 2nd rnd 10 (11) times = 58 (62) sts. Then work in pats as follows: Knit the right center st and 1 (2) sts, work in Openwork Pat over the following 25 sts, knit remaining sts. After 18 (19) cm/7 (7½)" from beg, for the Instep inc 1 st at each side of the center st every 2nd rnd 8 (9) times. And with the 3rd Instep increase, work the increase for the Heel every 2nd row 6 (7) times = 86 (94) sts. Then over the center

18 (20) sts of the Sole sts, work the Cap in St st. On both sides, knit the last or the first Cap st with one st from the side Sole sts together 14 (17) times = 58 (60) sts. Then for the Leg cont in pats as established over all sts for 2 rnds, and on the 1st rnd work SKP with the last Cap st and the following st and work knit 2 tog with the first Cap st and the previous st. Also, for the larger Size, dec 2 sts = 58 sts. Then over the Stockinette sts cont in Ribbing Pat for 3.5 cm/1½". Cont in Stripe Pat, working in Stockinette Stitch over the Openwork Pat. After 6 rows of Stripe Pat, knit 1 rnd with yellow, then work 7 rnds in Border Pat and bind off all st in pat.

Stitch Chart 1

Stitch Chart 2

Stitch Key

☐ = 1 knit st

☐ = 1 purl st

☐ = 1 yo

☐ = k2tog

☐ = SKP: slip 1 st, knit 1, pass the slipped st over knit 1

☐ = SK2P (= slip 1 st, knit 2 tog, pass the slipped st over k2tog)

Leaf Pattern Socks
Size: Adult 9/10 (Adult 10/11)

Materials:
200 g plum (75% Wool, 25% Polyamide, Yardage = 210 m/50 g), 1 set (5) dpn size 2.5 mm (US 1)

Stockinette Stitch in rnds: Knit every rnd.

Stockinette Stitch in rows: Knit sts on RS rows, purl sts on WS rows.

Reverse Stockinette Stitch in rnds: Purl every rnd.

Leaf Pat: multiple of 15 sts. Work following the Stitch Chart. Only the odd-numbered rnds are shown, on the even-numbered knit all sts, except

for garter st, purl the sts. Rep rnds 1–32.

Ribbing Pat: *1 st in Stockinette St, 1 st in Reverse Stockinette St; rep from *.

Gauge, Stockinette Stitch: 28 sts and 40 rows = 10 x 10 cm/4 x 4".

How to:
For the Toe with dpn, cast on 6 sts and work the Basic Course on pages 52–53 until there are 18 sts. Work in Stockinette St. For the extension, inc each side of 2 center sts (4 sts inc'd) every 2nd rnd 10 (11) times = 58 (62) sts. After 19 (20) cm/7½ (8)", for the Instep and the Heel inc 4 sts every 2nd rnd 7 (8) times = 86 (94) sts. Then over the center 18 (20) sts of the Sole sts, work the Cap in St st. On both sides, knit the last or the first Cap st with one st from the side Sole sts together 12 (16) times = 62 sts. Then for the Leg work in Stockinette Stitch over all sts, and on the 1st rnd work SKP with the last Cap st and the following st and work knit 2 tog with the first Cap st and the previous st = 60 sts. Then cont in Leaf Pat over all sts, working the stitch rep 4 times. After Leg measures 17 cm/6½" (be sure to end with either a 16th or 32nd rnd of the Stitch Chart), for the Cuff band work in Ribbing Pat for 5.5 cm/2", then bind off all sts loosely in pat.

Stitch Chart

Stitch Key

☐ = 1 knit st   ☐ = 1 yo

☐ = k2tog

☐ = SKP: slip 1 st, knit 1 pass the slipped st over knit 1

☒ = garter st (knit the odd-numbered rnds, purl the even-numbered rnds)

Socks with Texture Pattern
Size: Adult 9/10 (10/11)

Materials:
100 g turquoise (75% Wool, 25% Polyamide, Yardage = 210 m/50 g), 1 set (5) dpn size 2.5 mm (US 1), 1 button

Stockinette Stitch (St st) in rnds: Knit every rnd.
Stockinette Stitch in rows: Knit sts on RS rows, purl sts on WS rows.
Reverse Stockinette Stitch in rnds: Purl every rnd.
Texture Pat: multiple of 4 sts: Follow the chart. Only odd-numbered rnds are shown, on even-numbered rnds, knit the k sts and purl the p sts, and knit the yo's. Rep rnds 1–20.
Ribbing Pat: *2 sts in Stockinette St, 2 sts in Reverse Stockinette St; rep from *.

Gauge, Stockinette Stitch: 28 sts and 40 rows = 10 x 10 cm/4 x 4".

How to:
For the Toe, with dpn cast on 6 sts and work the Basic Course on pages 52–53 until there are 18 sts. Work in St st. For the extension, inc each side of 2 center sts (4 sts inc'd) every 2nd rnd 10 (11) times= 58 (62) sts. After 18 (19) cm/7 (7½)" above Toe, for the Instep inc 1 st at each side of the center st every 2nd rnd 8 (9) times. And with the 3rd Instep inc, work the inc for the Heel every 2nd row 6 (7) times = 86 (94) sts. Then over the center 18 (20) sts of the Sole sts, work the Cap in St st. On both sides, knit the last or the first Cap st with 1 st from the side Sole sts tog 12 (14) times = 62 (66) sts. Then for the Leg, cont in St st over all sts, and on the 1st rnd work SKP with the last Cap st and the following st and work knit 2 tog with the first Cap st and the previous st = 60 (64) sts. When Leg measures 1 cm/¼" cont in Texture Pat for 40 rnds. For the Cuff work in Ribbing Pat for 8 cm/3¼", then bind off all sts loosely. Fold cuff in half to RS.

Stitch Chart

I	I	↓	U	I	I	↓	U		19
U	I	I	I	U	I	I			17
↓	U	I	I	↓	U	I			15
U	⟋	I	I	U	⟋	—	—		13
⟋	I	I	I	U	⟋	—	—		11
I	I	U	⟋	I	I	U	⟋		9
I	I	⟋		I	I	⟋			7
I	I	—	—	I	I	—			5
I	I	—	—	I	I	—			3
I	I			I	I				1

└─ Rep ─┘

Stitch Key

I = 1 knit st	↓ = SKP: slip 1 st, knit 1, pass slipped st over knit 1
— = 1 purl st	
U = 1 yo	⟋ = k2tog

Bobble Socks
Size: Adult 9/10 (10/11)

Materials:
100 g olive (75% Wool, 25% Polyamide, Yardage = 210 m/50 g), 1 set (5) dpn size 2.5 mm (US 1), cable needle (cn)

Stockinette Stitch (St st) in rnds: Knit every rnd.
Stockinette Stitch in rows: Knit sts on RS rows, purl sts on WS rows.
Reverse Stockinette Stitch in rnds: Purl every rnd.
Texture Pat (over 18 sts): Follow Stitch Chart 1. Only the odd-numbered rnds are shown. On the even-numbered rnds, knit the k sts and purl the p sts, or as stated. Rep rnds 1–10.
Bobble Pat (over 11 sts): Work same as Texture Pat, but follow Stitch Chart 2.
Ribbing Pat: *1 st in Stockinette St, 1 st in Reverse stockinette St; rep from *.

Gauge, Stockinette Stitch: 28 sts and 40 rows = 10 x 10 cm/ 4 x 4".

How to:
For the Toe with dpn cast on 6 sts and work Basic Instructions on pages 52–53 until there are 18 sts. Work in Stockinette St. For the extension, inc each side of 2 center sts (4 sts inc'd) every 2nd rnd 10 times = 58 sts. Then work in pats as follows: Work right center st in Stockinette St, 5 sts in Stockinette St, 18 sts in Texture Pat, remaining sts in Stockinette St. After 18 (19) cm/7 (7½)" from beg, for the Instep inc 1 st at each side of the center st every 2nd rnd 8 (9). And with the 3rd Instep increase, work the increase for the Heel every 2nd row 6 (7) times = 86 (90) sts. Then over the center 18 (20) sts of the Sole sts, work the Cap in St st. On both sides, knit the last or the first Cap st with 1 st from the side Sole sts tog 13 (15) times = 60 sts. Then for the Leg cont in pats as established over all sts, and on the 1st rnd work SKP with the last Cap st and the following st and work knit 2 tog with the first Cap st and the previous st = 58 sts. When the 10th row of the Texture Pat has been worked, cont as follows: Cont in Texture Pat over the same sts as established and work 11 sts each side in Bobble Pat and the remaining 18 sts in Texture Pat. After 50 rnds from beg of Bobble Pat, for the Cuff work 9 cm/3½" in Ribbing Pat, then bind off all sts loosely in pat.

Stitch Key

I = 1 knit st	
⟋↗ = Cross 2 sts Right: slip 1 st to cn and hold to back of work, knit 1 and knit 2 from cn	
X = 1 st in garter st (knit odd-numbered rnds, purl even-numbered rnds)	
● = 1 bobble (work 5 sts in 1 st: knit 1, yo, knit 1, yo, knit 1; turn work, purl 5 sts, turn work, knit 5 sts together)	

Stitch Chart 1

X	X	I	I	I	I	⟋	I	I	I	I	I	I	I	⟋	I	X	X		9
X	X	I	I	I	⟋	I	I	I	I	I	I	⟋	I	I	X	X			7
X	X	I	I	⟋	I	I	I	I	I	I	⟋	I	I	I	X	X			5
X	X	I	⟋	I	I	I	I	I	I	⟋	I	I	I	I	X	X			3
X	X	⟋	I	I	I	I	I	I	⟋	I	I	I	I	I	X	X			1

Stitch Chart 2

I	I	X	X	X	X	X	I	I		9
I	I	X	X	I	X	X	I	I		7
I	I	X	X	X	X	X	I	I		5
I	I	X	X	I	X	X	I	I		3
I	I	X	X	●	X	X	I	I		1

With colorful yarn and a crochet hook, get started and crochet a pair of socks.

With beautiful finishing touches and pattern variations, the crocheted sock is like the knitted sock in every way.

Trends with a Hook

If you do not knit, or prefer to crochet, you'll find the right pair of socks in this chapter. On the next page, we describe the basic instructions on how it is done. Crocheted socks have high cuddle factor, but when crocheted with a thin yarn are also quite suitable for summer. You will find patterns for both large and small feet. The basic instructions for the socks begin on page 74.

Crochet lovers don't have to switch to knitting needles. Our crocheted socks are just as much fun to make!

Crochet hooks come in so many different styles...materials like metal and bamboo, hooks with a grip, or a reinforced plastic handle. You can get advice from knitting stores to find just the right hook for you.

The 4-Step Method
for crocheted socks

❶ Step—The Toe

The beginning is the same for all socks. For the tip of the toe, make a yarn ring and work 8 hdc into the ring, join the rnd with sl st in 1st st and follow Crochet Chart 1, working the corresponding number of rounds for the specified size. On the 2nd round double the sts to 16 sts. From the 3rd round, 4 sts are increased every round. Work back and forth in rounds, that is, turn at the end of every round. In this way, the beginning of the round does not move and the center of the sole is easily found. You can mark the right and left of the center stitch with a stitch marker or yarn marker.

❷ Step—The Foot, Heel & Instep

Now for the Foot continue to work even. For the foot length crochet as many rounds or cm/in as designated on the Size Table on page 143 or as stated in the Instructions. Keep moving the marker at the end of every round. Then for the Instep and Heel on every following rnd work 2 hdc before and after the right center st and before and after the left center st. Repeat these increases as many times as designated on the Size Table or as indicated in the Instructions.

❸ Step—The Cap

Work the Cap following Crochet Chart 2. The last increase round is a right-side round, after the turn, work slip st up to the end of the Cap st and go back 1 st over the side of the Heel edge, as shown, then turn work and continue to follow the Crochet Chart. The last increase rnd is a wrong-side rnd, first work slip st up the edge of the Cap and work 1 st over the side of the Heel edge, as shown, then turn work and continue to follow the Crochet Chart. On the 1st Cap row, work 2 single crochet together at beginning and end of row, on the following rows, work decrease only at the end of every row. To work this decrease, insert hook in the last st of the cap, yo and draw up a loop, then insert hook in the following st at the side of the Heel, yo and draw up a loop, yo and draw through all loops on hook. Then turn and work 1 single crochet in the last st, as shown. Continue to follow the Chart. The chart is shown over 15 sts, as indicated on the Size Table for sizes 8/9, 9/10 and 10/11. For smaller sizes, work fewer sts each side of the center sole st and for larger sizes work more sts. The corresponding number of rows is indicated on the Size Table or in the Instructions.

❹ Step—The Leg

The Leg begins at the end of the Cap—also with the 18th row of the Crochet Chart 2. Then for the shaping, depending on the size, work additional decrease as on rnds 19 and 20. This is described on the Size Table or in the instructions. Then the original number of sts that were on the Foot is again reached. Work the Leg length as described or to the desired length.

Left Sock: For socks with a lateral pattern on the Leg, work pattern in reverse after the Cap.

Crochet Charts for Foot and Heel

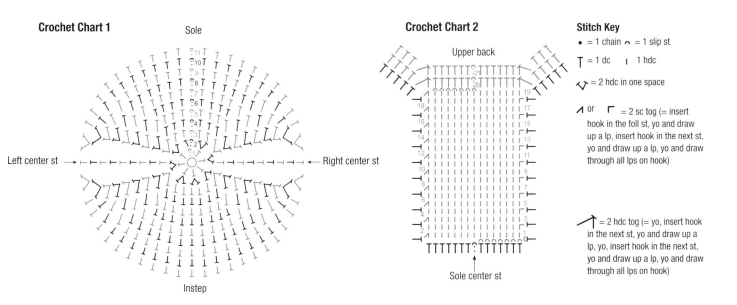

Crochet Chart 1

Sole

Left center st → ← Right center st

Instep

Crochet Chart 2

Upper back

Sole center st

Stitch Key

- = 1 chain ∩ = 1 slip st
- T = 1 dc ı 1 hdc
- ⋎ = 2 hdc in one space

∕ or Γ = 2 sc tog (= insert hook in the foll st, yo and draw up a lp, insert hook in the next st, yo and draw up a lp, yo and draw through all lps on hook)

⋀ = 2 hdc tog (= yo, insert hook in the next st, yo and draw up a lp, yo, insert hook in the next st, yo and draw up a lp, yo and draw through all lps on hook)

Crochet Stitches

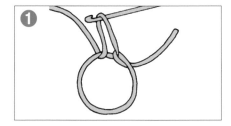

Yarn ring: Make a loop same as a slip knot and draw up a loop into this circle as shown. Through this loop work ch 2 = 1st hdc.

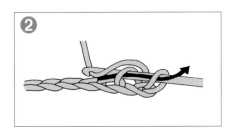

Slip Stitch (sl st): Insert hook into stitch (chain), yo and draw up through both loops on hook.

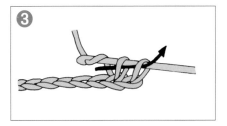

Single Crochet: Insert hook into stitch (chain), yo and draw up a loop, yo and draw through both loops on hook.

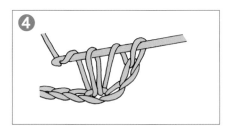

Half Double Crochet (hdc): Yo, insert hook into stitch, yo and draw up a loop, yo and draw though all loops on hook.

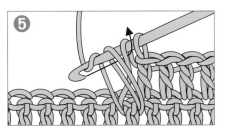

Front Post dc: Yo, insert hook from front to back to front around post of dc from row below, yo and draw up a loop, yo and draw through 2 loops, yo and draw through all loops on hook.

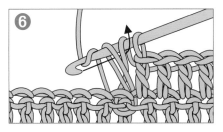

Back Post dc: Yo, insert hook from back to front to back around post of dc from row below, yo and draw up a loop, yo and draw through 2 loops, yo and draw through all loops on hook.

The Remedy
for Cold Feet

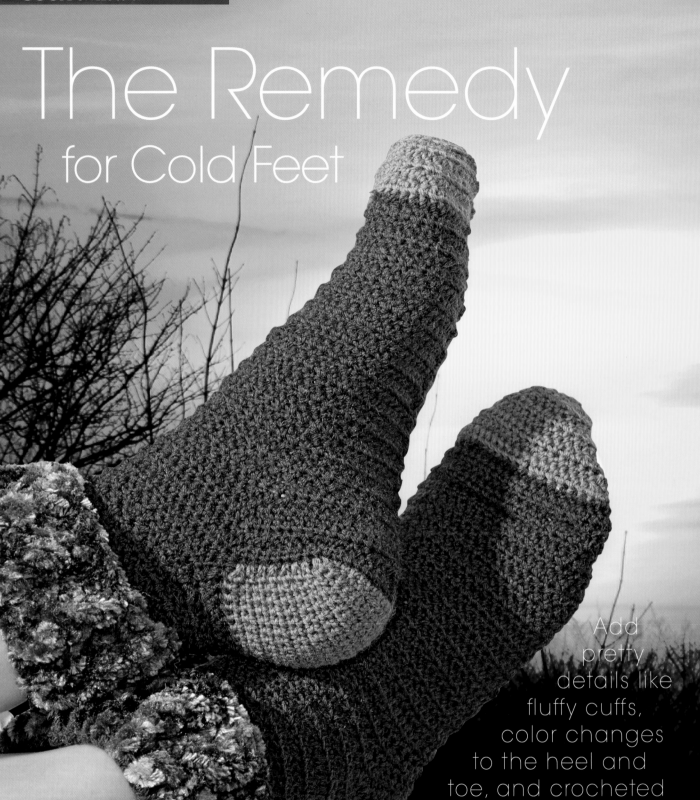

Add pretty details like fluffy cuffs, color changes to the heel and toe, and crocheted flowers to warm up the socks.

Colorful Socks
Size: Adult 9/10 (10/11)

Materials:
Approx 100 g pink mix and 50 g purple mix (75% Wool, 25% Polyamide, Yardage = 210 m/50 g), 1 crochet hook size 2.5 mm (US B/1)

Main Pat: Half double crochet, beg every rnd with ch 2 (which counts as 1st hdc) and join every rnd with 1 sl st in top of beg chain. After the 2nd rnd, turn work at end of every rnd.
Leg Pat: multiple of 3 sts. Follow the Crochet Chart working in the Main Pat. For clarity, the last rnd of the Main Pat is shown at the bottom of the chart. Rep rnds 1–3 once, then rep rnds 2 and 3 five times more. End by working rnds 4 and 5, and after the 4th

rnd, do not turn = 15 rnds in total.
Stripe Leg Pat: [2 rnds in purple, 2 rnds in pink] 3 times, then end with pink.

Gauge, in Main Pat: 23 hdc and 18 rows = 10 x 10 cm/4 x 4".

How to:
With pink make a yarn ring and work 8 hdc in ring, and follow the Basic Course on pages 70–71. For the toe, work 9 rnds = 44 sts. Cont in Main Pat, working 1 rnd purple, 2 rnds pink and 2 rnds purple, then cont in pink. When piece measures 17 (18) cm/6½ (7)" from beg, work 2 rnds in purple then

cont in pink for Heel and Instep, work increase each side of both center sts every rnd 6 times, working inc sts in Main Pat = 68 sts. Then work the Cap in purple over 15 sts and work back and forth in rows for 19 rows. For the Leg work 2 rnds in pink in Main Pat, working 4 increases as described = 44 sts. Then for the Leg work 15 rnds in Stripe Leg Pat, and on the 1st rnd, inc 1 st = 45 sts. After 15 rnds of Leg Pat, fasten off.

Crochet Chart

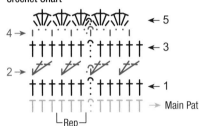

Stitch Key
- • = chain
- ⌒ = slip st
- ı = sc
- T = hdc
- † = dc

Work the sts grouped tog all in 1 stitch.

Socks with Flowers
Size: Adult 9/10 (10/11)

Materials:
100 g pastel mix (75% Wool, 25% Polyamide, Yardage = 210 m/50 g), crochet hook size 2.5 mm (US B/1)

Main Pat: Work hdc, begin each round with ch 2 which counts as the 1st hdc and join every rnd with 1 sl st in top of beg ch. At the 2nd rnd, turn work at end of every rnd.
Crochet Flower: Make a yarn ring and work 8 sc in ring. Join 1st rnd with sl st in the 1st sc, then work rnds 2 and 3 following Crochet Chart, on the 2nd rnd work through back loop only. For the inner

flower, join yarn to any st on the 1st rnd and working into the front loop, work 1 sc and 1 picot (= ch 3, 1 sc in the 1st ch) in each st around, Join rnd with 1 sl st in the 1st sc.

Gauge, in Main Pat: 23 hdc and 18 rows = 10 x 10 cm/4 x 4".

How to:
Make a yarn ring and work 8 hdc in ring, and follow the Basic Course on pages 70–71. For the Foot, work 9 rnds = 44 sts. Then work in Main Pat. After 18 (19) cm/7 (7½)" from beg, for Heel and Instep work increase each side of both center sts every rnd 6 times, working incs in Main Pat = 68 sts. Then work the Cap in purple over 15 sts and work back and forth in rnds for 19 rows, following the Basic Course. Then for the Leg work 2 rnds in Main Pat, working 4 incs as described = 44 sts. Then work 11 more rnds in Main Pat. For the top of the Leg work 1 rnd on RS as follows: ch 1, *1 sc in next st, ch 3, skip 1 st; rep from *, end with 1 sl st in 1st sc. Fasten off. From behind, join yarn in any slipped st, ch 1, *1 sc from behind in the next skipped st, ch 3, 1 sc from front of next skipped st, ch 3; rep from *. Join rnd with 1 sl st in the 1st sc.

Finishing:
Make 4 crochet flowers, 2 flowers with the inner flower and 2 flowers without the inner flower. Sew flower on to Legs as shown in photo, or as desired.

Crochet Chart

Stitch Key
- • = ch
- ⌒ = sl st
- ı = sc
- † = dc
- ⊥ = sc, working in back loop only

Socks with Cuffs
Size: Adult 8/9 (9/10)

Materials:
Approx 100 g each purple and fuchsia (75% Wool, 25% Polyamide, Yardage = 210 m/50 g), approx 50 g plush yarn in pink mix (Yardage = approx 45 m/50 g), 1 crochet hook size 2.5 mm (US B/1), 1 crochet hook size 5 mm (US H/8)

Main Pat: Work hdc, begin each round with ch 2 which counts as the 1st hdc and join every rnd with 1 sl st in top of beg ch. At the 2nd rnd, turn work at end of every rnd.

Border Pat: Over an even number of sts. On RS rnds, work *1 hdc, 1 fpdc (= yo, insert hook from front to back to front around post of the st from previous rnd and complete dc); rep from *. On WS rnds, work *1 hdc, bpdc (= yo, insert hook from back to front to back around post of the st from previous rnd and complete dc); rep from *.

Gauge, with purple or fuchsia and 2.5 mm (US B/1) hook in Main Pat: 23 hdc and 18 rows = 10 x 10 cm/4 x 4".

How to:
Make a yarn ring with fuchsia and work 8 hdc in ring, and follow the Basic Course on pages 70–71. For the Foot, work 8 (9) rnds = 40 (44) sts. Then work in Main Pat with purple. After 17 (18) cm/6½ (7)" from beg, for Heel and Instep work increase each side of both center sts every rnd 6 times = 64 (68) sts. Then work the Cap in fuchsia over 15 sts and work back and forth in rows for 19 rows. Then for the Leg cont in Main Pat with purple, and on the first 2 rnds work 4 sts increases as described. Over the remaining 40 (44) sts work 8 cm/3¼" more in Main Pat. Then for the Cuff, change to 5 mm hook and plush yarn and work in Border Pat, and on the 1st rnd, dec 20 (22) sts evenly spaced. After 5 cm/2" in Border Pat, fasten off. Fold band to outside.

Color-Mix Socks
Size: Adult 9/10 (10/11)

Materials:
Approx 100 g self-striping, purple color yarn (80% Wool, 20% Polyamide, Yardage = 210 m/50 g), 1 crochet hook size 2.5 mm (US B/1)

Main Pat: Work hdc, begin each round with ch 2 which counts as the 1st hdc and join every rnd with 1 sl st in top of beg ch. At the 2nd rnd, turn work at end of every rnd.

Leg Pat: Over an even number of sts. Follow Crochet Chart directly from the Main Pat. To help you better understand the pat, the last rnd of the Main Pat is shown at the bottom of the chart. Work rnds 1–4 once, then rep rnds 3 and 4 twice more. Then work rnds 5–9 once = 13 rnds in total.

Gauge, in Main Pat: 23 hdc and 18 rows = 10 x 10 cm/4 x 4".

How to:
Make a yarn ring with fuchsia and work 8 hdc in ring, and follow the Basic Course on pages 70–71. For the Foot, work 9 rnds = 44 sts. Then work in Main Pat. After 18 (19) cm/7 (7½)" from beg. For Heel and Instep, work increases each side of both center sts every rnd 6 times, working incs into Main Pat = 68 sts. Then work the Cap over 15 sts and work back and forth in rows for 19 rows following the Basic Course. Then for the Leg work 2 rnds in Main Pat, dec 4 sts = 44 sts. Then work 13 rnds in Leg Pat, then fasten off.

Crochet Chart

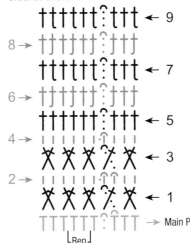

Stitch Key
- • = 1 ch
- ⌒ = 1 sl st
- ı = 1 sc
- T = 1 hdc
- † = 1 dc
- ⌡ = 1 fpdc (yo, insert hook from front to back to front around post of the st from previous rnd and complete dc)
- ⌠ = 1 bpdc (yo, insert hook from back to front to back around post of the st from previous rnd and complete dc)
- ✕ = Cross 2 dc (skip 1 st, dc in next st, dc in skipped st)

75

Yarn Just Feels Good

Pull on a
pair of
snuggly
slippers, put
up your feet,
and relax.
Here's how to
keep your feet
warm and cozy.

Crochet Inspiration

Crocheted socks of this kind can also be used as slippers, and are a convenient accessory for your guests.

For non-slip slipper soles you can apply stripes of latex caulking on the finished sole; after drying it will serve as a slip-resistant tread. Or, look for non-slip soles in knitting or sewing shops.

Slippers for Teens
Size: Child 7½/8 (8/8½) 9/9½

Materials:
Approx 150 (150) 200 g orange and 50 g natural (70% Acrylic, 30% Wool, Yardage = 55 m/50 g), 1 crochet hook size 7 mm (K/10½)

Main Pat: Work hdc, begin each round with ch 2 which counts as the 1st hdc and join every rnd with 1 sl st in top of beg ch. At the 2nd rnd, turn work at end of every rnd.

Gauge, in Main Pat: 22 hdc and 8 rows = 10 x 10 cm/4 x 4".

How to:
Make a yarn ring with orange and work 8 hdc in ring, and follow the Basic Course on pages 70–71. For the Foot, work 4 (5) 5 rnds, and for the middle size inc 2 sts on the last rnd = 24 (26) 28 sts. Then work 6 (6) 7 rnds in Main Pat. For Heel and Instep work increase each side of both center sts every rnd 3 times = 36 (38) 40 sts. Then work the Cap in orange over 9 (11) 11 sts and work back and forth in rows for 7 rows. Then for the Leg cont in orange in

Main Pat, dec 2 sts on the 1st and 2nd rnds as described = 24 (26) 28 sts. Fasten off. Leave the center Instep st unworked and for the Cuff, join natural in next st and work back and forth in rows in Main Pat for 3 rows, leaving the center front st unworked and inc 1 st each side every row. After the 3rd row, there are 29 (31) 33 sts. Fasten off.

Slippers for Men
Size: Adult 11/12 (14) 15

Materials:
Approx 200 (250) 250 g mocha and 50 g natural (70% Acrylic, 30% Wool, Yardage = 55 m/50 g), 1 crochet hook size 7 mm (K/10½)

Main Pat: Work hdc, begin each round with ch 2 which counts as the 1st hdc and join every rnd with 1 sl st in top of beg ch. At the 2nd rnd, turn work at end of every rnd.

Gauge, in Main Pat: 22 hdc and 8 rows = 10 x 10 cm/4 x 4".

How to:
Make a yarn ring with mocha and work 8 hdc in ring, and follow the Basic Course on pages 70–71. For the Foot, work 7 (8) 8 rnds, for the middle size inc 2 sts on the last rnd = 36 (38) 40 sts. Then work 9 (9) 10 rnds in Main Pat. For Heel and Instep work increase each side of both center sts every rnd 4 times = 52 (54) 56 sts. Then work the Cap over 13 sts and work back and forth in rows for 11 rows. Then for the Leg cont in Main Pat, dec 2 sts on the 1st and 2nd rnds as described = 36 (38) 40 sts.

Fasten off. Leave the center Instep st unworked and for the Cuff, join natural in next st and work back and forth in rows in Main Pat for 3 rows, leaving the center front st unworked and inc 1 st each side every row. After the 3rd rows, there are 41 (43) 45 sts. Fasten off.

Socks in Natural Tones
Size: Adult 9/10 (10/11)

Materials:
Approx 100 g natural (75% Wool, 25% Polyamide), Yardage = 420 m/100 g) and 50 g sand (90% Acrylic, 10% Mohair, Yardage = 140 m/50 g), 1 crochet hook in sizes 2.5 and 4 mm (US B/1 and G/6)

Main Pat: Work hdc, begin each round with ch 2 which counts as the 1st hdc and join every rnd with 1 sl st in top of beg ch. At the 2nd rnd, turn work at end of every rnd.
Stripe Pat: multiple of 2 sts: Follow Crochet Chart directly from the Main Pat. The last rnd of the Main Pat is shown at the bottom of the chart. Work rnds 1–5 once, then rep rnds 2–5, working in colors as noted at the side of the chart, working rnds 1, 2 and 5 with natural and 2.5 mm hook and rnds 3 and 4

with Sand and size 4 mm hook. When changing colors, work last lps of last st before color change with the new color.

Gauge, in Main Pat and natural: 23 hdc and 18 rows with 2.5 mm hook = 10 x 10 cm/4 x 4".

How to:
With 2.5 mm hook and natural, make a yarn ring. Work 8 hdc in ring, and follow the Basic Course on pages 70–71. For the Foot, work 9 rnds. After 18 (19) cm/7 (7½)" from beg, for Heel and Instep increase each side of both center sts every rnd 6 times = 68 sts. Then work Cap over 15 sts and work back and forth in rows for 19 rows. Then for Leg work 2 rnds in Main Pat, dec 2 sts on 1st and 2nd rnds as described = 44 sts. Then over all sts work in Stripe Pat. After 14 rnds in Stripe Pat, for the Cuff work 10 rnds in Main Pat, then fasten off.

Crochet Chart

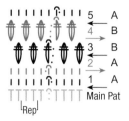

Stitch Key

- • = 1 ch
- ∩ = 1 sl st
- I = 1 sc   A = natural
- T = 1 hdc   B = sand

✿ = work 3-tr cluster in one space

Sock Fun
from Small to Large

The basic shape of the crocheted sock is very versatile and can be adorned with such things as fancy little buttons.

Handmade socks are something unique. With lovingly designed details, such as button embellishments or fancy cuffs, they become even more special.

The beautiful multicolor gradient comes directly from the ball of yarn.

Baby Socks
Size: Child 4/5 (5/6) 6/6½

Materials For each pair of socks in yellow and white: approx 25 g each white, yellow and orange (100% Wool, Yardage = 190m/50 g), 1 crochet hook size 2.5 mm (US B/1), 2 buttons

Main Pat: Work hdc, begin each round with ch 2 which counts as the 1st hdc and join every rnd with 1 sl st in top of beg ch. At the 2nd rnd, turn work at end of every rnd.

Gauge, in Main Pat: 23 hdc and 18 rows = 10 x 10 cm/4 x 4".

How to:
Make a yarn ring with white or yellow and work 8 hdc in ring, and follow the Basic Course on pages 70–71. For the Foot, work 4 (5) 5 rnds = 24 (28) 28 sts. Then cont in Main Pat. After 7 (8) 9.5 cm/2¾ (3¼) 3¾" from beg, for Heel and Instep work increase each side of both center sts as described every rnd 3 (3) 4 times = 36 (40) 44 sts. The work the Cap over 9 (9) 11 sts and work back and forth in rows for 9 rows. Then work the Leg in Main Pat, and on the 1st rnd dec 2 sts = 24 (28) 28 sts. After 9 rnds of the Leg have been worked (for the yellow socks, after 5 rnds cont in white) change to orange and work 1 rnd sc, then work next rnd as follows: 1 sc in the 1st st, *skip 1 st, 4 hdc in the next st, skip 1 st, 1 sc in the next st; rep from *, end with skip 1 st, 4 hdc in the next st, skip 1 st,1 sl st in the 1st sc. Fasten off. Fold Leg approx 3 cm/1¼" to outside and sew on button.

Socks with Fringed Leg
Size: Adult 9/10 (10/11)

Materials:
100 g yellow (75% Cotton, 25% Polyamide, Yardage = 210 m/50 g), 100 g fringe yarn in yellow (100% Polyester, Yardage = 80 m/50 g), 1 crochet hook size 2.5 mm (US B/1), 1 crochet hook size 3.5 mm (US E/4)

Main Pat: Work hdc, begin each round with ch 2 which counts as the 1st hdc and join every rnd with 1 sl st in top of beg ch. At the 2nd rnd, turn work at end of every rnd.

Stripe Pat: Over an even number of sts. Follow the Crochet Chart 1 directly from the Main Pat. The last rnd of the Main Pat is shown at the bottom of the chart. Work rnds 1–9 once, then rep rnds 4–9 twice more and end with rnds 8 and 9 once = 23 rnds. Turn work after each rnd.

Border Pat: Over an even number of sts. Follow Crochet Chart 2 in Cotton. Work rnds 1–4 once. Turn work after each rnd.

Gauge, in Main Pat with Cotton yarn and size 2.5 mm (US B/1) hook: 23 hdc and 18 rows = 10 x 10 cm/4 x 4".

How to:
Make a yarn ring with 2.5 mm hook and yellow and work 8 hdc in ring, and follow the Basic Course on pages 70–71. For the Foot, work 9 rnds = 44 sts. Cont in Main Pat. After 18 (19) cm/7 (7½)" from beg, for the Heel and Instep work increase each side of both center sts as described every rnd 6 times, working increases in Main Pat = 68 sts. Then work the Cap over 15 sts and work back and forth in rows for 19 rows. Then for the Leg work 2 rnds in Main Pat, dec a total of 4 sts as described = 44 sts. Then work the 23 rnds of the Stripe Pat once. For the Cuff, turn the work to the inside and work 1 rnd hdc, working in the back loops only. This rnd represents the rnd under the Crochet Chart 2. Work rows 1–4 of Border Pat once, then fasten off.

Crochet Chart 1

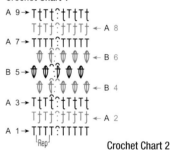

Crochet Chart 2

Stitch Key

- • = 1 chain
- ∩ = 1 slip st
- ι = 1 sc
- T = 1 hdc
- ⇕ = work 3 dc tog in one space

- ϯ = 1 fpdc (yo, insert hook from front to back to front around post of st from previous row and complete dc)
- t = bpdc (yo, insert hook from back to front to back around post of st from previous row and complete dc)
- J = 1 fphdc (yo, insert hook from front to back to front around post of st from previous row and complete hdc)
- ʈ = 1 bphdc (yo, insert hook from back to front to back around post of st from previous row and complete hdc)

- A = Cotton yarn with 2.5 mm hook
- B = Fringe yarn with 3.5 mm hook

Socks in Oranges
Size: Child 8/8½ (Adult 10/11)

Materials:
100 g orange mix (75% Wool, 25% Polyamide, Yardage = 210 m/50 g), 1 crochet hook size 2.5 m (US B/1)

Main Pat: Work hdc, begin each round with ch 2 which counts as the 1st hdc and join every rnd with 1 sl st in top of beg ch. At the 2nd rnd, turn work at end of every rnd.
Shell Pat: multiple of 8 sts. Follow the Crochet Chart directly from the Main Pat. The last rnd of the Main Pat is shown on the chart. Work rnds 1–5 once.

Gauge, in Main Pat: 23 hdc and 18 rows = 10 x 10 cm/4 x 4".

How to:
Make a yarn ring and work 8 hdc in ring, and follow the Basic Course on pages 70–71. For the Foot work 7 (9) rnds = 36 (44) sts. Then cont in Main Pat. After 13.5 (19) cm/5½ (7½)" from beg, for Heel and Instep work increases each side of both center sts as described every rnd 5 (6) times = 56 (68) sts. Then work the Cap over 13 (15) sts and work back and forth in rows for 15 (19) rows following the

Basic Course. Then for the Leg cont in Main Pat, working 4 decreases on the first 2 rnds as described = 36 (44) sts. When Leg measures 8 (10) cm/3¼ (4)" increase 4 sts evenly on the next rnd = 40 (48) sts. Then work 5 rnds in Shell Pat and fasten off.

Crochet Chart

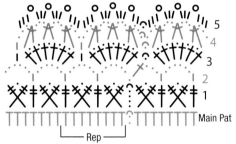

5
4
3
2
1
Main Pat
└── Rep ──┘

Stitch Key
- **•** = 1 chain
- **⌒** = 1 sl st
- **|** = 1 sc
- **†** = 1 dc
- **‡** = 1 tr
- **⋏** = 2 dc together
- **⤬** = cross 1 tr, 1 chain and tr (= skip 2 sts, work 1 tr in the next st, chain 1 and work 1 tr in the 1st skipped st)
- **o** = 1 picot (chain 3 and work 1 sc in the 1st chain)

Rainbow Socks
Size: Child 8/8½ (Adult 7/8) Adult 10/11

Materials:
100 g self-striping yarn in multi colors (75% Wool, 25% Polyamide, Yardage = 210 m/50 g), 1 crochet hook size 2.5 mm (US B/1)

Main Pat: Work hdc, begin each round with ch 2 which counts as the 1st hdc and join every rnd with 1 sl st in top of beg ch. At the 2nd rnd, turn work at end of every rnd.

Gauge, in Main Pat: 23 hdc and 18 rows = 10 x 10 cm/4 x 4".

How to:
Make a yarn ring and work 8 hdc in ring, and follow the Basic Course on pages 70–71. For the Foot work 7 (8) 9 rnds = 36 (40) 44 sts. Then cont in Main Pat. After 13.5 (16) 19 cm/5½ (6¼) 7½" from beg for Heel and Instep work increases each side of both

center sts as described every rnd 5 (5) 6 times = 56 (60) 68 sts. Then work the Cap over 13 (13) 15 sts and work back and forth in rows for 15 (15) 19 rows. Then for the Leg work in Main Pat, working 4 decreases = 36 (40) 44 sts. When leg measures approx 6 (8) 10 cm/2½ (3¼) 4", for the front Ruffle, working in front loop only, work 2 hdc in each st. Work the back ruffle in same way working into the back lp of each st.

Tip: If you want the color striping of each sock to be the same, begin the second sock with the same color section as the first sock.

Colorful Crochet Fun

Choose a multi-color for your crocheted socks to make them gorgeous and colorful. But you can also use a monochromatic yarn with a small touch of a second color, such as on the cuffs or as an accent.

WOODS of WINDSOR

Color effect
can be set very
specifically when
you're working in
crochet, either
using a self-striping
yarn or multiple
colors.

Socks with Post Stitch Pattern
Size: Child 8/8½ (Adult 10/11)

Materials:
Approx 100 g pink mix (80% Wool, 20% Polyamide, Yardage = 210 m/50 g), 1 crochet hook size 2.5 mm (US B/1)

Main Pat: Work hdc, begin each round with ch 2 which counts as the 1st hdc and join every rnd with 1 sl st in top of beg ch. At the 2nd rnd, turn work at end of every rnd.

Post Stitch Pat: multiple of 8 sts. Follow the Crochet Chart directly from the Main Pat. The last rnd of the Main Pat is shown at the bottom of the chart. Work rnds 1–8 once.

Gauge, in Main Pat: 23 hdc and 18 rows = 10 x 10 cm/4 x 4".

How to:
Make a yarn ring and work 8 hdc in ring, and follow the Basic Course on pages 70–71. For the Foot work 7 (9) rnds = 36 (44) sts. Then cont in Main Pat. After 13.5 (19) cm/5½ (7½)" from beg, for Heel and Instep work inc each side of both center sts as described every rnd 5 (6) times = 56 (68) sts. Then work the Cap over 13 (15) sts and work back and forth in rows for 15 (19) rows. Then for the Leg work 2 rnds in Main Pat, decrease 4 sts as described = 36 (44) sts. Cont in Post Stitch Pat until Leg measures approx 10 cm/4"—end with a chart rnd 7—fasten off.

Crochet Chart

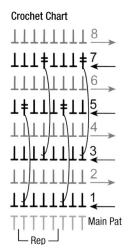

Stitch Key

⊥ = 1 sc, inserting hook in front loop of each st from previous rnd

‡ = 1 fpdc (yo, insert hook from front to back to front around post of st from 4 rnds below and complete dc)

Socks with Striped Cuffs
Size: Child 8/8½ (Adult 7/8) Adult 9/10

Materials:
Approx 100 g aubergine and 50 g rose (75% Wool, 25% Polyamide, Yardage = 210 m/50 g), 1 crochet hook size 2.5 mm (US B/1)

Main Pat: Work hdc, begin each round with ch 2 which counts as the 1st hdc and join every rnd with 1 sl st in top of beg ch. At the 2nd rnd, turn work at end of every rnd.

Stripe Pat: multiple of 3 sts. Follow Crochet Chart directly from the Main Pat. The last rnd of the Main Pat is shown at the bottom of the chart. Work rnds 1–3 once, then rep rnds 2 and 3, working the color changes.

Gauge, in Main Pat: 23 hdc and 18 rows = 10 x 10 cm/4 x 4".

How to:
Make a yarn ring with aubergine and work 8 hdc in ring, and follow the Basic Course on pages 70–71. For the Foot, work 7 (8) 9 rnds = 36 (40) 44 sts. Then work 1 rnd in Main Pat in rose, then cont in Aubergine. After 13.5 (16) 18 cm/5½ (6½) 7½" from beg, for Heel and Instep work increase each side of both center sts as described every rnd 5 (5) 6 times = 56 (60) 68 sts.
Then work the Cap over 13 (13) 15 sts and work back and forth in rows for 15 (15) 19 rows.
Then for the Leg cont in Main Pat, working the 4 decreases on the first 2 rnds as described = 36 (40) 44 sts.
When Leg measures 7 cm/2¾", for the Cuff, turn work and work 6 rnds in Stripe Pat, and on the 1st rnd 0 (dec 1 st) inc 1 st = 36 (39) 45 sts. Then fasten off.

Crochet Chart

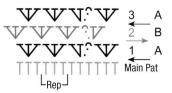

Stitch Key

• = 1 chain
⌒ = 1 sl st
T = 1 hdc
V̄ = 3 hdc in 1 st

A = Rose
B = Aubergine

Crocheted Baby Socks with Ruffle or Shell Pattern

Size: Child 4/5 (5/6) 6/6½

Materials:
For the Socks with Ruffle in fuchsia: approx 50 g fuchsia mix and approx 50 g fuchsia
For the Socks with yellow border: approx 50 g green mix and approx 50 g yellow (75% Wool, 25% Polyamide, Yardage = 210 m/50 g), 1 crochet hook size 2.5 mm (US B1)

Main Pat: Work hdc, begin each round with ch 2 which counts as the 1st hdc and join every rnd with 1 sl st in top of beg ch. At the 2nd rnd, turn work at end of every rnd.
Texture Pat: Over an even number of sts. *1 dc, 1 fpdc (yo, insert hook from front to back to front around post of st from row below and complete dc).
Crochet Border: multiple of 5 sts. Follow Crochet Chart in rnds directly into the last row of sock. Work rnds 1–4 once. For a better overview, the last row of sc is shown under the Crochet Chart.

Gauge, in Main Pat: 23 hdc and 18 rows = 10 x 10 cm/4 x 4".

How to:
Socks with Ruffle in Fuchsia
Make a yarn ring with fuchsia and work 8 hdc in ring, and follow the Basic Course on pages 70–71. For the Foot work 4 (5) 6 rnds = 24 (28) 32 sts. Then cont in Main Pat. After 7 (8) 9.5 cm/2¾ (3¼) 3¾" from beg, for Heel and Instep work increase each side of both center sts as described every rnd 3 times = 36 (40) 44 sts. Then work the Cap over 9 sts and work back and forth in rows for 9 rows. Then for the Leg cont in Main Pat, working the 4 decreases on the first 2 rnds as described = 24 (28) 32 sts. Then cont in Texture Pat. When Leg measures approx 4.5 cm/1¾", work 1 WS rnd in sc in fuchsia. Then for the Ruffle, ch 3, work 4 dc in each st around. Join with 1 sl st in top of beg chain.

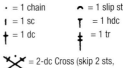

Socks with Yellow Shell Pat Border
Begin same as the Socks with Ruffles, but using green mix. When Leg measures 4 cm/1½", work 2 RS rnds and 1 WS rnd in sc with yellow, and on the 1st rnd increase 0 (2) 1 sts = 24 (30) 33 sts. Then work Shell Pat following Crochet Chart, and on the 2nd rnd increase 1 (0) 2 sts = 25 (30) 35 sts.

Crochet Chart

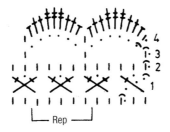

Stitch Key:
• = 1 chain   ⌒ = 1 slip st
| = 1 sc   T = 1 hdc
† = 1 dc   ‡ = 1 tr

✗ = 2-dc Cross (skip 2 sts, 1 dc in next st, ch 1, 1 dc in the skipped st)

In Refined Rounds

Knitting with 2 circular needles—try it out!
You'll quickly see the advantages and will
have fun while you knit.

These socks can be knit using 2 circular
needles following the Basic Course on pages
90–93 or the Basic Course on pages 8–9
and 40–41 with a set of double-pointed
needles. Use the Size Table on pages
142/143 for the desired size.

**You'll notice the benefits quickly, once
you have started:**

1. You save about three hundred interruptions as
compared to knitting with five needles. This
means **flexible knitting** with fewer needle
changes and without accidentally
dropping stitches! **2.** You can try on
the socks **at any time**; the needles
wrap around the Foot, and no
stitches fall off. **3.** You will
never have to look for a lost
needle that has dropped to
the floor and rolled under
the sofa—You can knit
relaxed and finish
quickly!

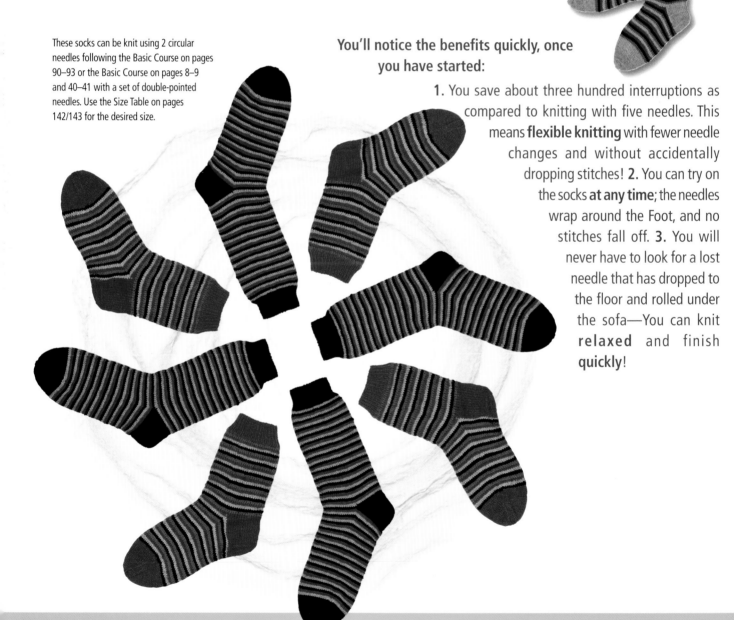

*Round and round—
have fun knitting!*

With beautiful yarn, anything knits up more
smoothly. Stop by your local yarn shop and
be inspired.

Socks Knit

with 2 circular needles

Small Sock Terminology: What's what in Sock Knitting
A = Cuff
B = Leg—worked as right-side and wrong-side rows
C = heel flap—enclosing the back Heel
D = Cap—sits under the Heel
E = Gusset—transition between Heel and Foot
F = Foot—knit in profile
G = Toe—knit together with the side stitches

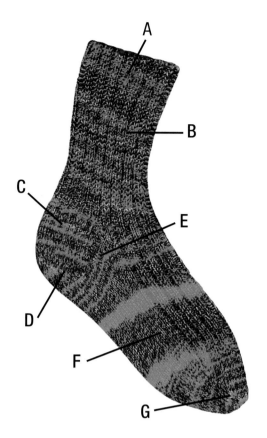

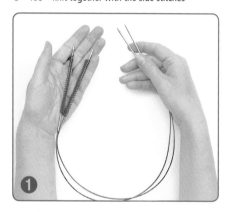

How to Start

1 Divide the cast-on stitches onto two circular needles. Place both needles next to each other in the left hand and push the stitches up to the tips of the needles. Be sure that the stitches are not twisted: The loops face outward, while the cast-on edge forms a long, narrow V between the needles.

2 For a join without a gap cross the first two stitches at beginning and end of the cast-on row. That is, slip the first stitch of the left needle to the right needle.

3 Subsequently, pass the first stitch on the right needle over the slipped stitch (see photo 3) and slip to the left needle. The working yarn comes from the middle of the joining. Casting on with two circular needles is much easier then using a set of double-pointed needles, where you have to struggle to keep the stitches untwisted and keep the join between the needles neat.

NOTES ON GAUGE

Usually when knitting in the round, the rows are knit a little tighter than when knitting back and forth in rows, so it is difficult to get the right stitches and rows over 10 cm/4". To take that gauge in the round, it goes like this: Cast on 63 stitches and join to work in the round. Then as in the tutorial, but with three circular needles in three different sizes, work 21 stitches on each needle in the designated pattern (usually Stockinette St). Place a maker every 21st stitch.

After you have knitted a swatch, you can count the stitches over 5 cm/2"; then double the calculated number—and it can be compared with what is given in the gauge in the Instructions. The needle size with the correct number of stitches for the gauge is the one to use for your socks. For the row gauge, it is usually sufficient to count the rows directly on the sock once you start knitting them.

Leg and heel flap

4 Pull out one of the two circular needles so far that the stitches are in the center of the wire—the needle points hang below. This needle is unused for the time being, while the stitches on the other needle (now the working needle) are being knit. With the free end of the working needle knit the stitches, then pull out the needle so far that these stitches are in the center of the wire. Now leave this needle unworked, it is also referred to as the 1st needle, since the first half of the stitches from the beginning of the round are on this needle. Turn the knitting and slide the stitches of the 2nd needle (now the working needle) to the end of the needle with the working yarn, and with the free needle, knit to the end of the round. Then pull out this needle so far that these stitches are in the center of the wire. Alternate working with both needles in this way, while working the **Cuff** and **Leg** following the respective instructions.

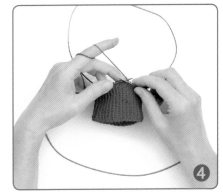

NOTE
Half the stitches are on each of the two circular needles. Only work with one needle at a time, working the stitches on one needle, then the other. Never use a needle to work sts from the other needle, because that's the secret: One needle works, the other one rests!

5 Here the entire **Leg** has been worked. Here you see how the non-working needle hangs behind the work in progress.

6 The **Heel Flap** is worked over the stitches on the first needle. The stitches on the second needle are for the Instep and remain unworked for now. The number of stitches (= heel flap width) and the number of rows (= heel flap depth) are stated on the Size Table on page 143. On RS rows, slip the first stitch knitwise, then alternate knit 1 stitch, slip 1 stitch with the yarn at back of work, and knit the last stitch of the row. On WS rows, slip the first stitch knitwise and purl all stitches to the last stitch, then knit the last stitch. Always end with a WS row.

Cap and Gusset

7 Work the round **Cap** in Stockinette Stitch (RS rows knit, WS rows purl). The stitch numbers of the Cap can be found on the Size Table on page 142. On the RS row, knit the last Cap stitch together with the following stitch, then knit 1 more stitch. Turn the work. On all WS rows, slip the 1st stitch purlwise and purl the last Cap stitch together with the following stitch (see photo 7), then purl the next stitch of the heel flap and turn the work again. On all RS rows, slip the first st knitwise. Continue in this way until all stitches have been used up. There are 2 more sts in every row.

8 From here on, continue knitting in the round and divide the sts again. Knit one WS row over the Cap stitches, working the first half with the previous working needle, the second half with the other needle. With this needle pick up 1 stitch in each edge stitch of the heel flap, pick up 1 st in the gap between heel flap and stitches on hold (mark this stitch), then knit half of the stitches on hold—follow the Basic Course. From here, with the first needle knit the second half of sts on hold, pick up 1 stitch in the gap (mark this stitch) and pick up 1 stitch in each edge stitch on the side of the heel flap, then work the first half of the Cap stitches. From here on, the sock can be seen in profile. The beginning of the round is at the center of the Sole. Work a second round, working the stitches of the Instep in designated patterns and knit the picked up stitches of the heel flap through the back loops and knit the remaining stitches.

NOTE

Depending on the pattern at the Instep, it may be necessary to maintain the stitch division from the Leg, that is, the stitches of the Instep remain on the 2nd needle, and the remaining stitches of the Heel or Sole on the 1st needle.

9 Then for the Gusset, decrease the stitches every 2nd round. For the left side of the heel flap, knit the marked stitch together with the stitch before (see photo 9), for the right side of the heel flap work SKP with the marked stitch and the stitch after (= slip the marked stitch knitwise, knit the next stitch, pass the slipped stitch over the knit stitch). Continue to work in this way until the original number of stitches from before the beginning of the Heel is reached.

Foot and Toe

10 Work the **Foot** as described in the instructions. For the foot length refer to the Size Table on page 142. It is measured from the beginning of the Cap to the beginning of the Toe.

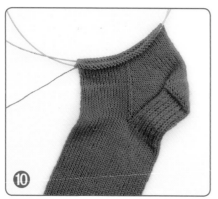

11 If the stitches have not been redistributed after the Heel, then it must be done now, so that the decreases for the **Toe** can be worked in the center of the needles. Work the Toe in Stockinette St. If there is an even number of sts, then dec the center 2 stitches on each needle on the next rnd so that there is an odd number on each needle. Then on every 2nd rnd, over the center 3 stitches on each needle work SK2P = slip 2 stitches as if to k2tog, knit 1 stitch, pass the 2 slipped stitches over the knit 1 (see photo 11). Rep these decreases every 2nd round until there are approx 11 stitches on each needle. Redistribute the stitches again so that the first 5 stitches of each needle are slipped to the other needle. Place both needles parallel side by side and join the stitches with Kitchener stitch.

Photos: ravek gesellschaft for bild-und datentechnik mbH

Thus the switch from double-pointed needles to circular succeeds!

When knitting with two circular needles, always alternate knitting from one needle to the other. It is important that you always use the needle where the stitches are located to knit these stitches. From the beginning, the front of the sock is on one needle, and the back side is on the other needle, so you do not have to redistribute the stitches for the Heel. You can work the Heel Cap according to your usual method or the method presented in this round Cap. The Gusset, when worked on double-pointed needles, is worked from the stitches at the beginning and end of each needle; when working with two circular needles, you mark the corresponding stitch at the transition from the Heel to the front of the Foot. So you can see exactly which stitches need to be knit together. In the round, in which the stitches are decreased from the heel flap, the stitches are redistributed, so now you can see the sock in profile. This allows the decreases for the Toe to take place in the center of the needle.

It looks especially beautiful when you weave the last stitches together using Kitchener stitch (see the tutorial below). To work this joining, you need to slip half of the stitches on each needle to the other, then place both needles parallel, side by side, and join them together as described.

If you prefer to draw the yarn through the remaining stitches, instead of weaving them together, then you should continue the decreases until a total of approx 10 stitches remains.

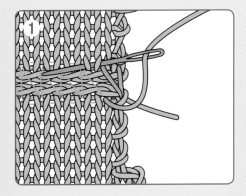

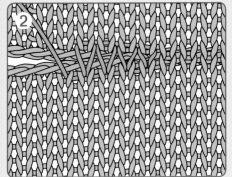

TIP

When sewing opposite stitches together with Kitchener stitch, a small point forms at both ends. There is a trick to prevent these jagged edges: Pass the outer stitch at each needle end over the adjacent stitch, so that 4 stitches, that would have looked uneven, are now neat. Now work the Kitchener stitch.

Kitchener Stitch

1 Place the needles parallel, side by side. Insert the needle through the last and the following stitch as shown, draw the yarn through, and drop the stitch from the needle.

2 On the opposite piece insert the needle through the last stitch and from below into the next st on needle, draw the yarn through and drop the stitch from the needle.

NOTE
You can also work other types of Toes, or draw the last stitches together with the end of the working yarn. If you choose this method, continue the decreases on every round until there are about 5 stitches on each needle. Cut the yarn and draw it through the remaining stitches and secure the end.

Short or Long

A fancy companion to ever-popular denim are multi-color socks in jeans shades…or, for fashionistas, extra-long ones with colorful stripes.

Knit Inspiration

Colorful stripes get tired legs kicking! With shorts, over the knee styles are particularly chic.

Cable Pattern Socks
Size: Adult 8/9 (9/10)

Materials:
Approx 100 g blue-gray-turquoise (45% Wool, 35% Cotton, 13% Polyamide, 7% Elité, Yardage = 230 m/50 g), 2 circular needles size 2.5 mm (US 1), 1 cable-needle (cn)

Cable Pat: multiple of 12 sts. Work following the Stitch Chart. Work rnds 1–34 once, then rep rnds 3–34.
Stockinette Stitch (St st): Knit sts on RS rows, purl sts on WS rows.
Slip St Pat: Rnd 1: *knit 1, slip 1 st knitwise, with yarn in back of work; rep from *; Rnd 2: Knit all sts. Rep rnds 1 and 2.

Gauge, Stockinette Stitch: 30 sts and 42 rows = 10 x 10 cm/4 x 4".

How to:
Cast on 60 sts and join to work in rounds (= 30 sts per needle). For the Leg work in Cable Pat for approx 16 cm/6¼" = 86 rnds. Leave the sts of the 2nd needle for the Instep on hold and cont over the remaining 30 sts of the 1st needle for the Heel following the Basic Course on pages 90–93. After 30 rows have been worked, work the Cap. For the Foot, cont again over all sts, do not redistribute the sts yet, but leave the 30 sts of Instep as well as the 52 sts of Heel for the Sole on one needle. Work the Instep sts in Cable Pat and the Sole sts in Slip St Pat. At the same time, work the decreases for the Gusset, that is, knit the first and last 2 sts of the Sole, until there are 60 sts again. Cont in pats as established until the foot measures 19 (20.5) cm/7½ (8)". Then redistribute the sts and work the Toe following the Basic Course, working in Stockinette St.

Stitch Key

☐ = 1 knit st
Ⅴ = slip 1 st purlwise with 1 yo
Ⓞ = Knit st together with yo
● = Purl st together with yo
[2 \ 3] = slip 2 sts to cn and hold to front of work, knit 3, then knit 2 from cn

Stitch Chart

(Stitch chart showing rows 1–34 with symbols, labeled "Repeat" at bottom)

Men's Socks
Size: Adult 10/11 (11/12)

Materials:
Approx 100 g blue-gray (45% Wool, 35% Cotton, 13% Polyamide, 7% Elité, Yardage = 230 m/50 g), 2 circular needles size 2.5 mm (US 1), 1 cable needle (cn)

Cable-Ribbing Pat: multiple of 16 sts or over 33 sts. Work following the Stitch Chart. Only the odd-numbered rnds/rows are shown. Work the even-numbered rnds/rows as knit the k sts and purl the p sts. On the Leg work rnds 1–28 of pat rep A, on rnds 29–52, work pat rep B, on Instep work all the 33 sts shown on chart. Work rnds 1–52 once, then rep rnds 5–52.
Stockinette Stitch (St st): Knit sts on RS rows, purl sts on WS rows.
Slip St Pat: Rnd 1: *knit 1 st, slip 1 st knitwise, with yarn in back of work; rep from *; Rnd 2: Knit all sts. Rep rnds 1 and 2.

Gauge, Stockinette Stitch: 30 sts and 42 rows = 10 x 10 cm/4 x 4".

How to:
Cast on 60 sts and join to work in rounds (= 30 sts per needle). For the Leg work in Cable Pat for approx 16 cm/6¼" = 86 rnds. Place the sts of 2nd needle for the Instep on hold and cont over the remaining 30 sts of the 1st needle for the Heel following the Basic Course on pages 90–93. After 30 rows work the Cap. For the Foot cont over all sts again, do not redistribute the sts yet, but leave the 30 sts of Instep as well as the 52 sts of Heel for the Sole on one needle. Continue the Instep sts in Cable Pat and work the Sole sts in Slip St Pat. At the same time, work the decreases for the Gusset, that is, knit the first and last 2 sts of the Sole, until there are 60 sts again. Cont in pats as established until the foot measures 21 (22.5) cm/8¼ (8¾)". Then redistribute the sts and work the Toe following the Basic Course, working in Stockinette St.

Stitch Chart on page 97

Stitch Chart

(chart with row numbers 1–51; Repeat B, Repeat A marked)

Stitch Key

☐ = 1 knit st ⊟ = 1 purl st

☑ = 1 knit st, working stitch in row below

Ⓤ = 1 yo

= knit 2 sts together

= SKP: slip 1 st knitwise, knit 1, then pass slipped st over knit 1

= purl 2 sts together

▲ = SK2P: slip 2 sts as if to k2tog, knit 1, then pass slipped sts over knit 1

= slip 4 sts to cn and hold to front of work, knit 5, then knit 4 from cn

Over the Knee
Size: Adult 8/9 (9/10)

Materials:
Approx 200 g pink-turquoise-pistachio (45% Wool, 35% Cotton, 13% Polyamide, 7% Elité, Yardage = 230 m/50 g), 2 circular needles size 2.5 mm (US 1)

Openwork Pat: multiple of 10 sts. Work following the Stitch Chart. Only the odd-numbered rnds are shown. Work the even-numbered rnds as knit the k sts and purl the p sts, and knit the yo's. Rep rnds 1–16.
Stockinette Stitch (St st): Knit sts on RS rows, purl sts on WS rows.

Gauge, Stockinette Stitch: 30 sts and 42 rows = 10 x 10 cm/4 x 4".
Gauge, Openwork Pat: 45 rnds = 10 cm/4".

How to:
Cast on 150 sts and join to work in rounds (= 75 sts per needle). Work the Leg in Openwork Pat for 15 rnds. For the Calf on the next rnd, dec 2 sts on the 1st needle, working SK2P (= slip 2 sts as if to k2tog, knit 1, then pass slipped sts over knit 1) over the center 3 sts. Rep this decrease every 12th rnd twice more, every 8th rnd 3 times and every 4th rnd 38 times, and alternate working the sts of the 2nd needle = 62 sts (= 31 sts per needle). Work even until approx 54 cm = 240 rnds in Openwork Pat have been worked. Leave the sts of the 2nd needle for the Instep on hold and cont over the remaining 31 sts of the 1st needle for the Heel following the Ba-

sic Course on pages 90–93, and on the 1st row decrease 1 stitch = 30 Heel sts. After 30 rows of Cap, cont over the center 10 sts. For the Foot, work again over all sts. There are 41 or 42 sts over two needles. At the Instep cont the center 31 sts in Openwork Pat and work remaining sts in Stockinette St. At the same time, work the Gusset, until there are 61 sts again. Cont in pats as established until Foot measures 19 (20.5) cm/7½ (8)". Then work the Toe in St St, and on the 1st rnd dec 1 st over the Openwork Pat = 60 sts (= 30 sts per needle).

Tip: If desired, weave elastic thread through the top edge to keep the stockings secure.

Stitch Chart
(chart with rows 1–15; Repeat marked)

Stitch Key
☐ = 1 k st ⊟ = 1 p st
Ⓤ = 1 yo
= knit 2 sts together
= SKP: slip 1 st knitwise, knit 1, then pass the slipped st over knit 1

Romantic

Even "big girls" like to wear rose and pink socks. In combination with small eyelet patterns, these socks look super with a little skin showing through.

and Sweet

Pink is the right color for this look. Pretty details and a basketweave pattern define the surface. For little boys, there is of course a different color.

My First Shoes

Openwork Pattern Socks
Size: 8/9 (Adult 9/10)

Materials:
Approx 100 g pink (45% Wool, 35% Cotton, 13% Polyamide, 7% Elité, Yardage = 230 m/50 g), 2 circular needles size 2.5 mm (US 1).

Openwork Pat: multiple of 10 sts. Work following the Stitch Chart. Rep rnds 1–4.

Stockinette Stitch (St st): In rows: Knit sts on RS rows, purl sts on WS rows; in rnds: Knit every rnd.

Gauge, Stockinette Stitch: 30 sts and 42 rows = 10 x 10 cm/4 x 4".

How to:
Cast on 60 sts and join to work in rounds (= 30 sts per needle). For the Leg work 19 cm/7½" in Openwork Pat. Leave the sts of the 2nd needle for the Instep on hold and work over the remaining 30 sts of the 1st needle for the Heel following the Basic Course on pages 90–93. After 30 rows, work the Cap. For the Foot, continue again over all sts. There are 41 sts on each of the 1st and 2nd needles. Continue the last 15 sts of the 1st needle as well as the first 15 sts of the 2nd needle for the Instep in Openwork Pat and work remaining sts in St St. At the same time, work the Gusset until there are 60 sts again. Cont in pats as established until Foot measures 19 (20.5) cm/7½ (8)". Then work the Toe in Stockinette St.

Stitch Chart

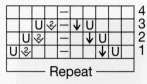

Stitch Key:
□ = 1 k st	⊟ = 1 p st

U = 1 yo

⊘ = knit 2 sts together

↓ = SKP: slip 1 st knitwise, knit 1, then pass the slipped st over the knit 1

Eyelet Pattern Socks
Size: Adult 8/9 (9/10)

Materials:
Approx 100 g rose (45% Wool, 35% Cotton, 13% Polyamide, 7% Elité, Yardage = 230 m/50 g), 2 circular needles size 2.5 mm (US 1), 1 crochet hook size 2.5 mm (US B/1)

Openwork Pat: multiple of 6 sts. Work following the Stitch Chart. Rep rnds 1–8.

Stockinette Stitch (St st): Knit sts on RS rows, purl sts on WS rows; in rnds, knit every rnd.

Gauge, Stockinette Stitch: 30 sts and 42 rows = 10 x 10 cm/4 x 4".

How to:
Cast on 60 sts and join to work in rounds (= 30 sts per needle). For the Leg work 18 cm/7" in Openwork Pat. Leave the sts of the 2nd needle for the Instep on hold and work over the remaining 30 sts of the 1st needle for the Heel following the Basic Course on pages 90–93. After 30 rows, work the Cap. For the Foot continue again over all sts, do not redistribute the sts yet, but leave the 30 sts of the Instep as well as the 52 sts of the Heel for the Sole on one needle. Cont the sts at the Instep in Openwork Pat and work remaining sts in Stockinette st. At the same time, work the Gusset until there are 60 sts. Cont in pats as established until Foot measures 19 (20.5) cm/7½ (8)". Then redistribute the sts and work the Toe in Stockinette st.
With crochet hook, work 1 rnd sc evenly along top edge of sock (be sure to work multiple of 6 sts) then work 1 rnd of shell pat as follows: ch 1, *skip 2 sts, work 5 dc in the next st, skip 2 sts, 1 sc in next st; rep from *, end with 1 slip st in the beg ch-1.

Stitch Chart

↓	U					8
	↓	U				7
		↓	U			6
			↓	U		5
			U	⊘		4
		U	⊘			3
	U	⊘				2
U	⊘					1

— Repeat —

Stitch Key:

□ = 1 knit st

U = 1 yo

⊘ = k2tog

↓ = SKP: slip 1 st knitwise, knit 1, then pass the slipped stitch over knit 1

Baby Booties in White-Rose
Size: 3–6 months,
Approx 8.5 cm/3½" foot length

Materials:
Approx 100 g white as well as 50 g each or a small amount in pink and rose (45% Wool, 35% Cotton, 13% Polyamide, 7% Elité, Yardage = 230 m/50 g), 2 circular needles size 3 mm (US 3), approx 1 m/1 yd Satin ribbon in white, 6 mm wide

Stockinette Stitch (St st): Knit sts on RS rows, purl sts on WS rows; in rnds knit every rnd.
Garter st: Knit every row; in rnds, alternate knit 1 rnd and purl 1 rnd.
Eyelet Rnd: *knit 2 tog, 1 yo; rep from *. Knit next rnd, including the yo's.
Slip St Pat: multiple of 2 sts. Rnd 1: With white knit all sts; Rnd 2: With white, purl 1, yo, *purl 2, yo; rep from *, end purl 1; Rnd 3: With pink, *knit 1, drop yo, slip 1 purlwise, with yarn in back of work; rep from *; Rnds 4 and 5: With pink, *purl 1, slip 1 purlwise, with yarn in back of work; rep from *; Rnd 6: With white, knit all sts; Rnd 7: With white *yo, purl 2; rep from *; Rnd 8: With rose, *drop yo, slip 1 purlwise, with yarn in back of work, knit 1; rep from *; Rnds 9 and 10: With rose, *slip 1 purlwise, with yarn

in back of work, purl 1; rep from *; Rnds 11–16: Rep rnds 1–6.

Gauge, Stockinette Stitch: 30 sts and 42 rows = 10 x 10 cm/4 x 4".

How to:
For the 1st Rolled Edge with rose cast on 40 sts and divide sts over 2 circular needles, join to work in rounds (= 20 sts per needle). Work 12 rnds in Stockinette st, then place the sts on hold. Work a 2nd Rolled Edge in pink same as the 1st edge, working 8 rnds in Stockinette st. Place the 2nd Rolled Edge over the 1st and with white, knit 1 st from each needle together and continue in this way until all sts are joined. For the Leg, with white work 5 rnds in garter st (beginning with a purl rnd), work 2 rnds Stockinette st, 1 Eyelet Rnd and 2 rnds Stockinette st. Work the following 10 sts of the 1st needle, then place these 10 sts and the 20 sts of the 2nd needle on hold. Over then remaining 10 sts for the Foot Flap work 22 rows garter st. For the Foot continue again over all sts, knit 1 rnd and along each edge of the Foot Flap, pick up 12 sts = 64 sts (= 32 sts per needle). Divide sts so that the shoe half is on one needle and you can see the Booties in profile. Then purl 1 rnd, work 16 rnds in Slip St Pat and purl

1 rnd, knit 1 rnd. Then continue the Sole in garter st, beginning with 1 purl rnd. For the Sole decreases, mark the 6th and 6th-to-last sts on each needle, then dec 1 st each side of marked sts every 2nd rnd 5 times as foll: work to 1 stitch before the marked sts, k2tog (that is the st before and the 1st marked st), then k2tog (that is with the 2nd marked st and the next st) = 40 sts. Join the Sole sts with Kitchener st. Cut satin ribbon in half and weave through the Eyelet Rnd on Leg.

Baby Booties in Gray-Blue
Size: 3–6 months,
Approx 8.5 cm/3½" foot length

Materials:
Approx 100 g gray as well as 50 g or a small amount in blue (45% Wool, 35% Cotton, 13% Polyamide, 7% Elité, Yardage = 230 m/50 g), 2 circular needles size 3 mm (US 3)

Stockinette Stitch (St st): Knit sts on RS rows, purl sts on WS rows
Garter st: Knit every row; in rnds 1 alternate knit 1 rnd and purl 1 rnd.
Eyelet Rnd: *K2tog, yo; rep from *. Knit next rnd, including the yo's.
Slip St Pat: multiple of 2 sts. Rnd 1: With gray knit all sts; 2nd Rnd: With gray, purl 1, yo, *purl 2, yo; rep from *, end purl 1; Rnd 3: With blue, *knit 1, drop yo, slip 1 purlwise, with yarn in back of work; rep from *; Rnds 4 and 5 With blue, *purl 1, slip 1 purlwise, with yarn in back of work; rep from *; Rnd 6: With gray, knit all sts; Rnd 7: With gray, *yo, purl 2; rep from *; Rnd 8: With blue, *drop yo, slip 1 purlwise, with yarn in back of work, knit 1; rep from *; Rnds 9 and 10: With blue, *slip 1 purlwise, with

yarn in back of work, purl 1; rep from *; Rnd 11–16: Rep rnds 1–6.

Gauge, Stockinette Stitch: 30 sts and 42 rows = 10 x 10 cm/4 x 4".

How to:
With gray cast on 40 sts and join to work in rounds (= 20 sts per needle). For the Rolled Edge work 10 rnds in Stockinette st. For the Leg work 10 rnds garter st, 2 rnds Stockinette st, 1 Eyelet Rnd and 2 rnds in Stockinette st. Knit the following 10 sts of the 1st needle, then place these 10 sts and the 20 sts of the 2nd needle on hold. Over the remaining 10 sts for the Foot Flap work 22 rows garter st. For the Foot continue again over all sts, knit 1 rnd and along each side of the Foot Flaps pick up 12 sts = 64 sts (= 32 sts per needle). Divide sts so that the shoe half is on one needle and you can see the Booties in profile. Purl 1 rnd, work 16 rnds in Slip St Pat and purl 1 rnd, knit 1 rnd. Then continue the Sole in garter st, beginning with 1 purl rnd. For the Sole decreases, mark the 6th and 6th-to-last sts on each needle, then dec 1 st each side of marked

sts every 2nd rnd 5 times as foll: work to 1 stitch before the marked sts, k2tog (that is the st before and the 1st marked st), then k2tog (that is with the 2nd marked st and the next st) = 40 sts. Join the Sole sts with Kitchener st. With blue make a twisted cord with a finished length of approx 50 cm/19½" long for each bootie and weave through the Eyelet Rnd on Leg.

addi♥-Express Socks

Almost unbelievable, but possible—socks knit with the popular mini-knitting machine! Try it out, and knit socks for the entire family in no time.

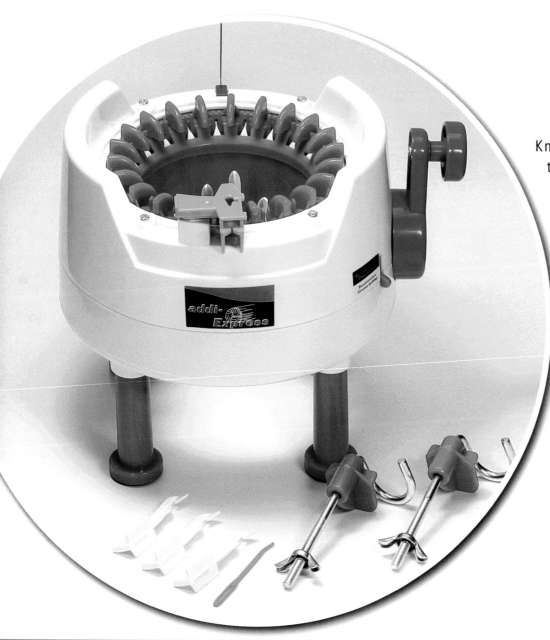

Knitting made easy—the Addi-Express knitting machine makes it possible. Simply turn the crank and in next to no time the socks are ready. Follow the instructions on pages 104–105, and knit the socks using the Basic Course on pages 104–107.

Knitting with the Addi-Express goes very quickly. The base is knitted in the round as a tube. It is the same form as with a sock worked with 2 needles or a set of double-pointed needles. You need knitting needles to make the Heel and Toe. The Cuff edging can be knitted or crocheted. For the Two-Color Socks here, you can see that the base is worked in violet and the Heel and Toe are worked in yellow.

These socks can be knit following the Basic Course on pages 104–107. For your desired size refer to the Size Table on page 107.

The yarn for socks knit with the Addi-Express needs to be a bit stronger. One with a yardage of about 70 m per 50 g is ideal. Superwash yarns are easy to machine wash, so are ideal for socks.

Basics for Knitting with the

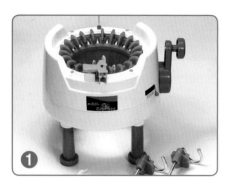

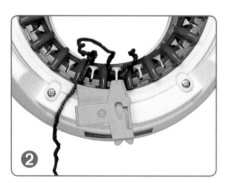

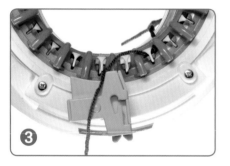

Plain Knitting

❶ First of all, switch the power button up to "Plain Knitting." Now crank the lever counter-clockwise to the cast on. Now the yellow needles protrude upwards. Roll about 20 cm/8" from a ball of yarn and place the beginning thread in the middle of the Addi-Express—it should be long enough to at least touch the table.

❷ Crank the handle back a little, clockwise—until the first white needle points to the left of the three top yellow ones. Then place the yarn around the first white needle. The three yellow needles are not used when working plain knitting, they merely indicate by stopping that they must be rotated in the opposite direction.

❸ Continue to turn the crank handle clockwise slowly and insert the yarn in the first row alternating front to back behind the ascending needles.

❹ The last needle, around which the yarn is running, is the first yellow needle. (This stitch later falls again and is pulled tight.) Bring the yarn at end of the first row to the outside. Now the yarn is inserted as with circular knitting (Photos 5 and 6) into the thread guide.

❺ In contrast to circular knitting, during straight knitting the crank is rotated clockwise from front to back. The row is finished as soon as the crank can no longer move. Note: Make sure to turn to the max! At the beginning of each row pull the yarn a bit, then the edge stitch will not be too loose.

❻ Work the bind off as in circular knitting (Photos 8 to 10).

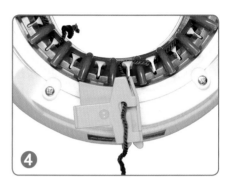

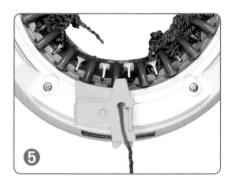

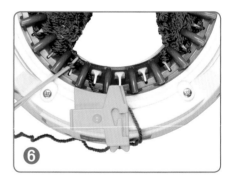

TIP
When a narrow side (cast-on stitches) hits a long side (edge stitches), alternate one stitch with one row and sew one stitch over every two rows. When rows meet, then sew row to row. The transition of two bound-off edges are the neatest when joined (before binding off) together to the open stitches with Kitchener stitch.

TIP
When working with a tape yarn, the yarn must be held at an angle so that the needles pick up the entire strand. You can work without the thread guide so that the yarn can be manually rotated. Always run the yarn loosely through the hand.

Addi-Express

Knitting in the round & joining

Before beginning to knit, set the power switch down to "Circular Knitting."

❶ Keep turning the crank to the right of the three yellow needles that protrude above. Now roll approx 20 cm/8″ of yarn from the ball and place the beginning of the strand in the middle of the Addi Express Knitting Machine—it should be long enough to touch the table. Bring the working yarn from right to left around the right of the yellow knitting needle.

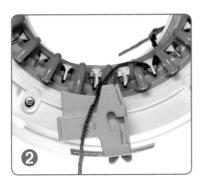

❷ Now slowly turn the crank clockwise with your right hand. With the left hand lay the yarn from front to back around the ascending needle. The yarn lies like a wave around the needles.

❸ Continue this process until the beginning of the round is reached. At the beginning of the round, bring the yarn to the outside.

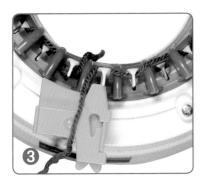

❹ Open the thread guide by pushing it to the left. Then place the working yarn from inside to outside of the thread guide.

❺ Before continuing, close the thread guide over the working yarn. Then hang the working yarn into the eye of the thread holder (not seen in this photo).

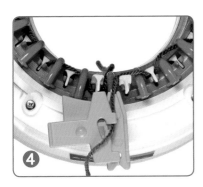

❻ Now turn the crank slowly and evenly clockwise. If turned too fast the needles may not grab the yarn. Never turn if there is resistance! The turning should go quite easily. If the stitches are too loose on the needles, simply pull evenly on the knitted piece from below with your left hand.

❼ Once the desired length of the knitted piece is reached, bind off: Cut the strand approx 30 cm/12″ long. Open the thread guide, take out the yarn, and thread it into the plastic needle.

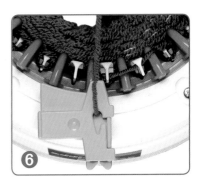

❽ With the plastic needle, thread the row clockwise stitch for stitch. For this purpose, lift the stitches between the red hooks of the Addi-Express, turning the crank slowly. Gently pull the knitted piece upward with the left hand.

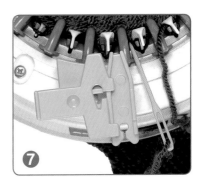

Socks Knit in the

① With the Addi-Express make a **knitted tube** approx 30 cm/12" long following the Basic Course on page 105. The length depends on the foot length plus the desired Leg length. Drop the finished knitting from the machine. Secure the open stitches with stitch holders.

② From the beginning of the tube, the **Cuff** will be knit first. For the **Rolled Edge** roll the fixed beginning strand to the outside and sew loosely with the initial beginning strand. It is very simple, looks good, and remains elastic. Other variations of the Cuff can be found in the instructions.

③ Lay the tube with the Cuffs flat, and **mark the Heel** position according to the desired length. At this marker, with a pair of small scissors, cut the lower thread of one stitch.

④ First, **unravel the strand** in the upper left corner of the stitch and place the free stitch on a needle. In the course of taking the strand completely out of the stitch, loosen the opposite st between the rows. Place this stitch on a 2nd needle.

⑤ Continue to unravel the stitches and place on the opposite needles until there are **10 stitches on each needle**. The strands at the sides will be used later for sewing.

⑥ For safety, first mark the right stitch on the lower needle, so that the beginning of the row is always visible.

Combined Technique

7 Then for the **Heel** work in Stockinette st. On the 1st round, inc 4 stitches evenly spaced around = 28 stitches in total. Work the Heel over 12 rounds, and on the 4th, 7th, 10th and 12th rounds, at the beginning of each needle work SKP (slip 1 stitch knitwise, knit 1 and pass the slipped stitch over the knit 1) with the 2nd and 3rd stitches, at the end of the rnds, work knit 2 together with the 2nd and 3rd to last stitch.

8 Continue these decreases until there are 12 stitches on each needle. Place 6 stitches opposite each other and join them with **Kitchener stitch** (see page 93).

9 Lay the knitted sock flat and determine the length from the Heel to the beginning of the Toe based on the desired **Size** (also refer to the table under step 10 here). Remove the stitch holders, and if necessary unpick the stitches and place on two needles, so there are 11 stitches on each needle, one for the Sole and the other for the Foot flap.

10 For guidance on the sock size and the length from the Heel to the beginning of the Toe, refer to the **Table** at right.

11 For the **Toe** mark the beginning of the round and on the first round, inc 1 st on each needle = 24 stitches in total.

12 Then work **the Band Toe** following the Basic Course on page 11. Divide the stitches over 4 needles with 6 stitches on each needle and every 2nd round decrease stitches until there are 8 stitches. Divide these stitches over 2 needles and join together with Kitchener stitch (see page 93).

10

Sock Sizes

Size	Length to the start of the Toe
Adult 8	18 cm/7"
Adult 8/9	19 cm/7½"
Adult 10	20 cm/8"
Adult 10/11	21 cm/8¼"
Adult 11/12	22 cm/8½"
Adult 14	23 cm/9"

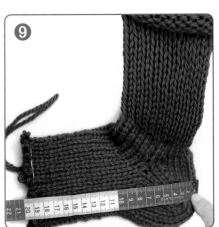

Snazzy Socks

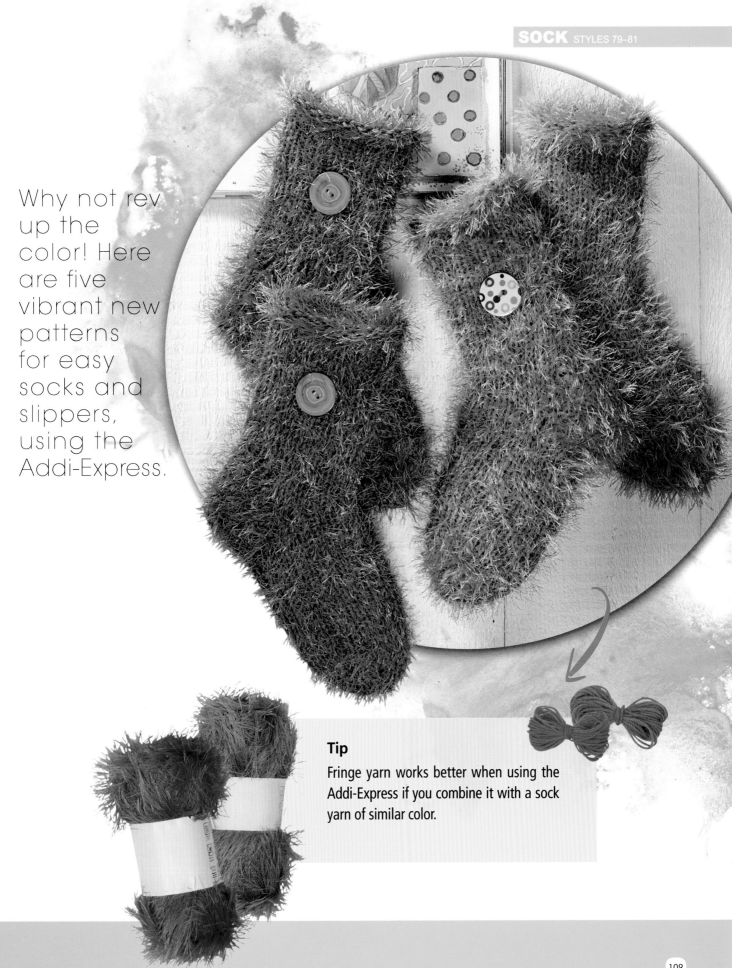

Why not rev up the color! Here are five vibrant new patterns for easy socks and slippers, using the Addi-Express.

Tip

Fringe yarn works better when using the Addi-Express if you combine it with a sock yarn of similar color.

Socks with Pompons

Size: Adult 8

Materials:
Approx 100 g orange, approx 50 g pink (98% Merino, 2% Polyester Elité, Yardage = 70 m/50 g), Addi-Express machine, 1 set (5) dpn size 5 mm (US 8), 1 crochet hook size 5 mm (US H-8), pompon maker

Stockinette Stitch (St st): In rnds, knit every rnd.
Crochet Edge: Work into the open cast on sts.
Rnd 1: *1 sc in next open st, ch 2; rep from * around, join with sl st in first st.
Rnd 2: 1 sc in 1st ch-2 sp of Rnd 1, *ch 2, 1 picot (ch 3, 1 sc in the 1st ch), ch 1, 1 sc in next ch-2 sp; rep from *, end with sl st in first st.

Gauge, Stockinette Stitch: 12 sts and 20 rnds = 10 x 10 cm/4 x 4".

How to:
Following the Basic Course on pages 104–107 work the basic form of the socks in orange with Addi-Express. Work the Cuff, Heel and Toe in pink with dpn or crochet hook. For the Cuff band, undo the cast-on edge and work the Crochet Edge into the open sts.

Finishing:
With the pompon maker, make 2 pompons (3 cm/1¼" in diameter) and attach 1 pompon to each sock's crochet edge.

Socks with Tassels

Size: Adult 8

Materials:
Approx 100 g green, approx 50 g turquoise (98% Merino, 2% Polyester Elité, Yardage = 70 m/50 g), Addi-Express machine, 1 set (5) dpn size 5 mm (US 8), 1 crochet hook size 5 mm (US H-8)

Stockinette Stitch: In rnds knit every rnd.
Knit edge: Work into the open cast-on sts.
Rnd 1: *K1, k in front and back of next st (to inc 1 st); rep from * = 32 sts.
Rnd 2: Purl.
Rnd 3: Knit.

Rnd 4: Knit.
Rnd 5: *K2tog, yo; rep from *.
Rnd 6: Knit all sts and yo's.
Rnd 7: Knit.
Rnd 8: Bind off sts very loosely purlwise.

Gauge, Stockinette Stitch: 12 sts and 20 rnds = 10 x 10 cm/4 x 4".

How to:
Following the Basic Course on pages 104–107, work the basic form of the socks in green with Addi-Express. Work the Cuff, Heel, and Toe in turquoise with dpn. For the Cuff band, undo the cast-on edge and work the band into the open sts .

Finishing:
With hook and green make two chains approx 50 cm/20" long and sl st into each ch. Weave the ties through the eyelet rnds of the knitted piece. Make and attach a 5 cm/2" tassel at the end of each tie.

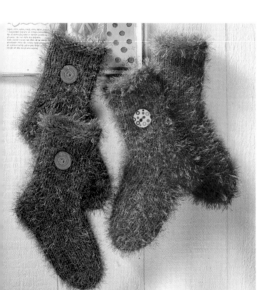

Fringe Yarn Socks in Turquoise or Pink

Size: Adult 9

Materials:
Approx 100 g fringe yarn in turquoise or pink (100% Polyester, Yardage = 90 m/50 g), approx 50 g sock yarn in turquoise or pink (75% Wool, 25% Polyamide, Yardage = 210 m/50 g), Addi-Express machine, 1 set (5) dpn size 5 mm (US 8), 1 crochet hook size 5 mm (US H-8), 4 colorful buttons

Stockinette Stitch: In rnds, knit every rnd.

Gauge, Stockinette Stitch: 12 sts and 20 rnds = 10 x 10 cm/4 x 4".

How to:
Following the Basic Course on pages 104–107 work the basic form of the socks with the Addi-Express using turquoise or pink, working 1 strand each of the fringe and sock yarn of the same color held together throughout.

Finishing:
Let the top edge roll to the outside and sew in place with some sock yarn of the same color. Sew a button to the outer Leg.

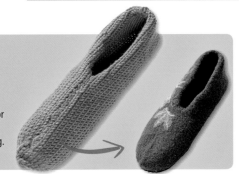

BEFORE & AFTER

Felted Slipper Basic Form

Follow the Basic Course on page 104 for the Basic Form of the Slipper in one piece in rows using the Addi-Express to the desired foot length. Then follow the instructions for sewing together and for the Toe decreases—and you are finished.
The photo shows the slipper before and after felting.

Green, Gray, or Violet Slippers
Size: Adult 10

Materials:
Approx 150 g each green, gray or violet (100% Wool, Yardage = 50 m/50 g) Addi-Express machine, some wool for needle felting in yellow green, leaf green and brown or in orange, yellow, red, some fringe yarn in violet-blue, Addi-Quick, finished soles

Stockinette Stitch: Knit sts on RS rows, purl sts on WS rows, in rnds knit every rnd.

Gauge, Stockinette Stitch: before felting 13 sts and 18 rnds = 10 x 10 cm/4 x 4", after felting 16 sts and 24 rows = 10 x 10 cm/4 x 4".

How to:
Following the Basic Course on page 104 work the basic form of the Slippers in green, gray or violet with the Addi-Express. Put the long sides together. Sew the narrow sides using the beginning strand. Sew the top together from the center to the other narrow side. For the Toe pick up the open sts and knit them together with both selvage sts = 32 sts. For the Toe, knit every 7th and 8th sts together. Rep these decreases every 5th rnd. Place decreases over each other. When 8 sts remain, draw yarn through the sts. With crochet hook, around the top opening of the violet slippers work with 2 rnds sc loosely using the fringe yarn.

Felting and Finishing:
Wash the slippers along with the main wash in the washing machine at 40°C/104°F and using liquid detergent. While slipper are still wet, pull into shape, stuff with newspaper, and let dry. Using the Addi-Quick felting machine decorate the green slippers with green leaves and yellow-green veins, and brown tendrils, following photo or as desired. For the gray slippers make motifs in orange, red, and yellow. For the violet slippers pull the fringed edge in shape. Sew on finished soles.

Felted Slippers in Pink and Yellow
Size: Adult 8

Materials:
Approx 150 g each pink or yellow (100% Wool, Yardage = 50 m/50 g), Addi-Express machine, small amount of wool yarn in yellow, red and blue, 1 pompon maker, approx 2 m/2 yd white satin ribbon (5 mm wide), finished soles

Stockinette Stitch: Knit sts on RS rows, purl sts on WS rows, in rnds knit every rnd.

Gauge, Stockinette Stitch: before felting 13 sts and 18 rnds = 10 x 10 cm/4 x 4", after felting 16 sts and 24 rows = 10 x 10 cm/4 x 4".

How to:
Following the Basic Course on page 104 work the basic form of the Slippers in pink or yellow with the Addi-Express. Put the long sides together. Sew the narrow sides using the beginning strand. Sew the top together from the center to the other narrow side. For the Toe pick up the open sts and knit them together with both selvage sts = 32 sts. On the next rnd knit every 7th and 8th sts together. With crochet hook, around the top opening work 2 rnds in dc, working loosely.

Felting and Finishing:
Wash the slippers along with the main wash in the washing machine at 40°C/104°F and using liquid detergent. While slippers are still wet, pull into shape, stuff with newspaper, and let dry. For the pink slippers, weave the ribbon through the dc edge. For the yellow slippers, with the wool yarn, make a twisted cord approx 50 cm/20" long in each color and weave through the top of the slipper. Make 2 pompons (3 cm/1¼" diameter) and sew to each end of the cord. Sew on finished soles.

On Tiptoes

A wellness program for your feet—felted slippers that adapt to the shape of your foot. Plus, these custom-made luxuries are found nowhere else!

Tip

Before the slippers dry completely, put them on so that they will shape to your foot. Then they will fit perfectly after they're dry.

Details can easily be needle felted onto the piece. Pull apart the wool yarn strand and place it on the already felted fabric. The piece should be on a padded surface. Now with the felting needle, jab the wool, with several strokes, into the felted fabric. You can place another layer of yarn over it, repeating until the underlying layer is completely covered.

Feel at Home:
Felted Slippers

Handmade and perfectly form-fitting. Slipping these on in the morning, or after a long day at work, makes being home even cozier.

Felted slippers can be crocheted, as described in the Basic Course on the next page. However, they can also be easily knit, as described in Chapter 5. In either case, they are felted in the washing machine. The fabric is made very loosely so that when felted in the machine the slipper shrinks to the desired size. You can personalize the slippers with decorations such as rhinestones, buttons, flowers, or felt details.

Be prepared:
Everyone will want a pair!

The washing machine does it!

The general nature of a felting yarn allows it to be felted in the washing machine through moisture, heat, and friction. When a crocheted or knitted piece is felted in the machine at 40°C/104°F in a full wash cycle with liquid detergent, it will shrink about 30%. Fill up the washing machine with towels or clothes of similar color. You can also add tennis balls to the load for extra friction.

Felting yarn must be 100% wool and have no superwash qualities in order to felt well in the washing machine. Wool yarn is available in many colors, of course...the possibilities are endless!

clic

How to Crochet Slippers

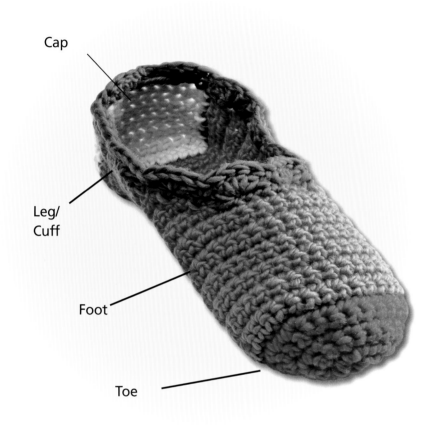

Cap

Leg/
Cuff

Foot

Toe

With our course and
the Size Table on
page 143 many of
these patterns can be
worked in any size. This
allows you to pamper
yourself and your
loved ones effortlessly
with handmade
felted slippers.

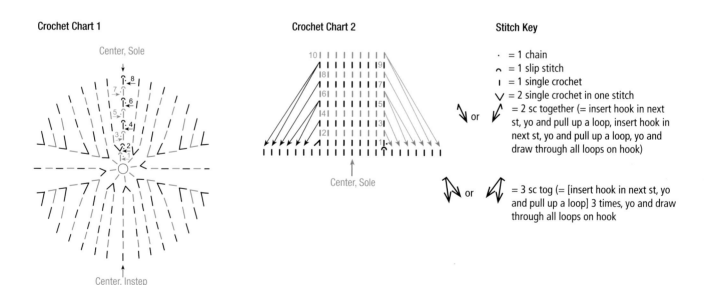

Crochet Chart 1

Center, Sole

8
7
6
5
4
3
2
1

Center, Instep

Crochet Chart 2

10
8   9
6   7
4   5
2   3
1

Center, Sole

Stitch Key

· = 1 chain

⌒ = 1 slip stitch

I = 1 single crochet

∨ = 2 single crochet in one stitch

↓ or ⋀ = 2 sc together (= insert hook in next st, yo and pull up a loop, insert hook in next st, yo and pull up a loop, yo and draw through all loops on hook)

⋀ or ⋀ = 3 sc tog (= [insert hook in next st, yo and pull up a loop] 3 times, yo and draw through all loops on hook)

Right Slipper
Step 1—Toe

The beginning is the same for all patterns. Unless otherwise stated, the pattern is worked in single crochet. For the Toe point, make a yarn ring and work 8 sc in the ring. Join the round with a slip st in the 1st st and following Crochet Chart 1 work the specified number of rounds for the respective size. On the 2nd round, work 2 sts in each st to double the sts = 16 stitches. From the 3rd round, work back and forth in rnds, that is, turn the work at end of every round. This is necessary so that the beginning of the round does not move and is always in the middle of the Sole, or later, the Foot. The 1st stitch after turning forms the center stitch of the sole of the foot. Directly opposite is the center stitch of the Instep. The increases are worked around these two center stitches. If according to the Table fewer sts are needed than at the 8th rnd of the Crochet Chart, then only work as many rounds as necessary until the desired number of stitches is reached. If the pattern requires a number of sts that is not divisible by 4, but 4 sts + 2 extra, on the last increase round, work only the 2nd and 3rd increase of the Crochet Chart.

Step 2—Foot and Heel

Now continue to work even for the Foot. Work the Foot opening for as many rounds as indicated in the Table or as stated in the Instructions, then work the increases for the Instep as indicated. After the end of the last increase round, fasten off. Now determine the center stitch of the Instep, join the yarn in this stitch and continue to work back and forth in rows. Work the decreases for the Foot every 2nd row according to the Table or as stated in the Instructions. Work the decrease each side, working the first and last 2 stitches together. For the Instep work increases every 2nd row according to the Table or as stated in the Instructions. Later, work the increases each side for the Cap stitches.

Step 3—Cap

Work the Cap following Crochet Chart 2. That is, after the last increase row of the Instep, fasten off and join yarn in the middle of the 1st Cap stitch. Work the Cap over the specified stitches. On the 1st Cap row, at the end of the row, work the last Cap stitch together with the following stitch. At the end of the following wrong-side row, work the last Cap stitch together with the following st. Continue to work decreases on the following right side and wrong side rows. On the right side row, work the last Cap stitch together with the following 2 stitches and on the following wrong side row, work the last Cap stitch together with the next 2 stitches. *On the next right and wrong side rows, work the last Cap stitch together with the following stitch, on the next right and wrong side rows, work the last Cap stitch together with the next 2 sts; rep from * until all the side sts are used up. Fasten off.

Step 4—Cuff/Leg

Join the yarn in the middle of the Cap or as specified and work 1 round single crochet around the foot. Fasten off to finish the piece, or work the Leg/Cuff as indicated in the Instructions.

Note: If you are not using a different color for the border, turn the work after the last Cap row, ch 1 and crochet around the opening.

Left Slipper
For patterns where the outer and inner side are different, then work the patterns in reverse.

Felt the slippers according to the instructions, shape, and let dry.

Whether large or small, everyone
needs to warm their cold feet,
and will enjoy handmade slippers.
They can be easily adapted to
whatever specifications you need.
(And the felted slippers in the
form of an animal are sure to
delight children of any age.)

By the Fireside

You can opt for bright colors or furry animals. In any case, it's fun to make slippers and decorate them in your own creative way.

Ballerinas with Ankle Strap
Size: Child 8/8½ (Adult 7/8) Adult 9/10

Materials:
Approx 200 g felting yarn in rainbow colors (100% Wool, Yardage = 50 m/50 g), 1 crochet hook size 7 mm (US L-11), 2 flower buttons in red, 2 felt buttons in green

Gauge single crochet: Before felting approx 14 sts and 18 rows = 10 x 10 cm/4 x 4". After felting 11 sts and 12 rows = 10 x 10 cm/4 x 4".

How to:
Right Ballerina: Beg the piece following the Basic Course

on pages 116–117 and continue as follows:
Step 1: For the Toe increase to 24 (26) 28 sts, but without increases on the 3rd, 5th and 7th rnds.
Step 2: After 10 (12) 12 rnds from beg (= after a right side round) fasten off and determine the center st of the Instep. Join the yarn on the following wrong side row at 2 sts from the center st of the Instep at the inside (= before and after the center st leave 2 sts unworked) and work 19 (21) 23 sc. On the following right side row, for the Foot opening, work the first and last 2 sts together = 17 (19) 21 sts. After 18 (22) 26 rnds/rows from beg, for the Instep, work 2 sc in the 4th (5th) 6th st and the 4th to last (5th to last) 6th to last st. Repeat these increases in the same place every row 1 (1) 2 times more = 21 (23) 27 sts.
Step 3: Work the Cap over 7 (7) 9 sts and 10 (12) 14 rows.
Step 4: For the Cuff, work around the top edge. Work Ankle Strap as follows: With a new length of yarn, join to the last Cap stitch and chain 21 (23) 25. Fasten off. With the working yarn join to the 1st Cap stitch and chain 7 (8) 9. Work sc in 2nd ch from hook and in each ch to end = 6 (7) 8 sc, work sc over the 7 (7) 9 Caps sts, and work sc over the 21 (23) 25 extra chain = 34 (37) 42 sts. Cont in sc for 4 rows. Work buttonloop on next row as follows: Work to the last 6 sts, ch 3, skip 3 sts, work to end.

Then work over all sts, working 3 sc in ch-3 lp, for 3 rows more. Fasten off.
Left Ballerina: Work same as Right Ballerina, but work the Ankle Strap in reverse as foll: Join the extra length of yarn on the last Cap stitch and ch 7 (8) 9 and at the 1st Cap stitch ch 21 (23) 25. Complete to correspond to Right Ballerina.

Felting and Finishing:
Felt the Ballerinas in the washing machine, pull in shape, and let dry. Sew button to Ankle Strap and felted button to Foot (see photo).

Ballerinas with Strap
Size: Child 8/8½ (Adult 7/8) Adult 9/10

Materials:
150 g felting yarn in green (100% Wool, Yardage = 50 m/50 g), 1 crochet hook size 7 mm (US L-11), 6 small flower buttons in yellow, 2 large flower buttons in yellow

Gauge single crochet: Before felting approx 14 sts and 18 rows = 10 x 10 cm/4 x 4". After felting 11 sc and 12 rows = 10 x 10 cm/4 x 4".

How to:
Right Ballerina: Beg the piece following the Basic Course on pages 116–117 in green and continue as follows:
Step 1: For the Toe work increases to 24 (26) 28 sts, but without increases on the 3rd, 5th and 7th rnds.
Step 2: After 10 (12) 12 rnds from beg (= after 1 right side round) fasten off and determine the center st of the Instep. Join the yarn on the following wrong side row at 2 sts from the center st of the Instep at the inside (= before and after the center st leave 2 sts unworked) and work 19 (21) 23 sc. On the following right side row, for the Foot opening, work the first and last 2 sts together = 17 (19) 21 sts. For the Strap, after 12 (14) 18 rnds/rows from beg, chain 16 (18) 20 + 1 for turning and work sc over all 33 (37) 41 sts. On the following right side row for the button loop work to the last 5 sts, ch 3, skip 3 sts, work to end. Then work over all sts, working 3 sc in ch-3 lp. Then leave the Strap sts unworked

and cont over the remaining 17 (19) 21 sts for 18 (22) 26 rnds/rows from beg. For the Instep work 2 sc in the 4th (5th) 6th st and in the 4th to last (5th to last) 6th to last. Repeat these increases in the same space 1 (1) 2 times = 21 (23) 27 sts.
Step 3: Work the Cap over 7 (7) 9 sts and 10 (12) 14 rows.
Step 4: To finish the top edge of the Strap, work as described in the Basic Course. To form the transition to the Strap work 2 sc together, in the corner of the Strap work 3 sc in 1 st.
Left Ballerina: Work same as the Right Ballerina, but work the Strap in reverse as foll: After 12 (14) 18 rnds/rows from beg join the extra strand to the 1st st and chain 16 (18) 20 + 1 for turning, then fasten off. Complete the Ballerina in reverse.

Felting and Finishing:
Felt the Ballerinas in the washing machine, pull in shape, and let dry. Sew 3 small flower buttons to the top of the foot and 1 large button to the Strap, using photo for placement, or as desired.

Sly Fox
Size: Adult 10

Materials:
200 g felting yarn in russet, 50 g in white and a small amount in black (each 100% Wool, Yardage = 100 m/50 g), 1 crochet hook size 7 mm (US L-11), 1 felting needle

Gauge single crochet: Before felting approx 14 sts and 18 rows = 10 x 10 cm/4 x 4". After felting approx 11 sts and 12 rows = 10 x 10 cm/4 x 4".

How to:
Step 1: Beg the piece following the Basic Course on pages 116–117, working the Toe in black = 8 sts. Continue in white as follows: Rnds 2 and 3: Work in sc; Rnd 4: 1 sc in next st, 2 sc in next st, 1 sc and 1 hdc in next st, 2 hdc in next st, 1 sc in next st, 2 hdc in next st, 1 hdc and 1 sc in next st = 14 sts; Rnds 5 and 8: Work in sc; Rnd 6 Work 5 sc, [2 hdc in next st] twice, 1 hdc, [2 hdc in next st] twice, work 4 sc = 18 sts. After the 6th rnd cont in russet. Rnds 7 and 9: Inc 4 hdc in the same place as the previous increases = 26 sts. Rnd 10 - 18: Work even in sc.
Step 2: On the 19th row, rejoin the yarn leaving the center st and 1 st after free, join in next st and work 23 sc, leave the st before the center st free. Rnd 20:

Work in sc. Rnd 21: Work the decreases for the Foot Opening = 21 sts. Rnds 22–26: Work in sc. Rnd 27 and 28: Inc 1 st each side of the center 7 sts = 25 sts. Rnds 29: Work in sc.
Step 3: Work the Cap over 7 sts and 14 rows.
Step 4: Work the top edge as described on the Basic Course on 116–117.

Ears (make 2): With russet chain 3 and follow the Crochet Chart rows 1–7.

Felting and Finishing:
Felt the pieces in the washing machine, pull in shape, and let dry. With white yarn, needle felt the inner ears following photo. Sew on ears. Needle felt the eyes in white, the pupils in black and the snout in russet, following photo. For the inner ears, eyes, and snout, cut short wool threads, twirl around each other, and needle felt. For the pupils cut one short strand and needle felt a small spot.

Crochet Chart

```
    7 ⊼ ˙. 7
  6 · T T T ⊼
    T T T T ∶ 5
  4 ∶ T T T T
    ⊺⊺ V ⊼ ˙. 3
  2 ˙. T T V
      V ˙. 1
```

Stitch Key
- · = 1 chain
- T = 1 hdc
- V = 2 hdc in 1 stitch
- ⊼ = 2 hdc together

Children's Slippers with Ears
Size: Child 6½/7 (7½/8) 8/8½

Materials:
200 g felting yarn in light brown and dark brown (100% Wool, Yardage = 50 m/50 g), 1 crochet hook size 7 mm (US L-11), 1 felting needle

Gauge single crochet: Before felting approx 14 sts and 18 = 10 x 10 cm/4 x 4". After felting approx 11 sts and 12 rows = 10 x 10 cm/4 x 4".

How to:
Step 1: For the Toe point follow the Basic Course on pages 116–117 in dark brown and work 8 sc into a yarn ring, join the rnd with slip st in the 1st st. On the 2nd rnd work 2 sc in each st. On the 3rd rnd increase to 20 (20) 22 sts, and after the 4th rnd change to light brown and work even.
Step 2: For the Instep, after 8 (10) 10 rnds from beg, on the following wrong side round, work 2 sc in the 7th (7th) 8th st and in the 6th to last (6th to last) 7th to last st. Rep these increases in the same place on the following 2nd rnd once more = 24 (24) 26 sts. After 12 (14) 14 rnds from beg (= after a right side rnd) fasten off and

determine the center st of the Instep. On the next wrong side rnd, rejoin the yarn from the inside leaving the center st and 1 st after free, join in next st and work 21 (21) 23 sc, leave the st before the center st free. For the Foot Opening, work the first 2 and last 2 sts together every following 2nd row once = 19 (19) 21 sts. After 16 (18) 18 rows from beg, for the Instep work 2 sc in the 6th (6th) 7th st and 6th to last (6th to last) 7th to last. Rep these increases in the same place, every 2nd row once more = 23 (23) 25 sts.
Step 3: Work the Cap over 7 sts and 12 (12) 14 rows.
Step 4: Finish the top edge as described in the Basic Course.

Ears (make 2): With dark brown make a yarn ring and work following the Crochet Chart.

Felting and Finishing:
Felt the pieces in the washing machine, pull in shape, and let dry. Sew on ears. Needle felt the eyes, nose, and mouth. For the eyes and nose, cut short wool threads, twirl around each other, and needle felt. For the mouth use one strand and needle felt around, little by little.

Crochet Chart

Stitch Key
- · = 1 chain
- ⌒ = 1 sl stitch
- I = 1 sc
- T = 1 hdc
- † = 1 dc

The symbols grouped tog at the bottom represent sts worked in 1 stitch.

Show Us Your Feet!

What you can do with these felted foot warmers! Create a classic in shades of blue, or make a pair of dolphins...these ideas can get you started on more of your very own.

Feel-Good Inspiration

Dolphin Slippers
Size: Adult 8/9

Materials:
200 g felting yarn in gray (100% Wool, Yardage = 50 m/50 g), 1 circular needle size 8 mm (US 11), 1 set (5) dpn size 8 mm (US 11), 4 small blue flat-back crystals to glue, jewelry stone adhesive

Stockinette Stitch (St st) in rnds: Knit every rnd.
Stockinette Stitch in rows: Knit sts on RS rows, purl sts on WS rows.

Gauge Stockinette Stitch: Before felting 12 sts and 19 rows = 10 x 10 cm/4 x 4". After felting 17 sts and 25 rows = 10 x 10 cm/4 x 4".

How to:
With circular needle, cast on 28 sts and work in Stockinette st for 28 rows. Then divide the sts over 4 dpn and join to work in rounds, and in the center front, cast on 2 new sts. Work in St st for 24 rnds. For the **Toe**, work k2tog with the last 2 sts of the 1st and 3rd needles, and the first 2 sts of the 2nd and 4th needle every rnd, until there are 3 sts on each needle. Work 5 rnds over the remaining 12 sts, then work k2tog around, cut yarn and draw through 6 sts together and stuff.
For the right **Flipper** (front flipper) cast on 7 sts over one dpn and work in Stockinette St for 3 rows, then at beg of every knit row, work k2tog, until there are 4 sts on needle. K2tog twice, then pass the 1st st over 2nd st and fasten off.
For the **Fin** (back flipper) cast on 20 sts to one dpn. On every row, work k2tog at beg of row and SKP at end of row. Fold into a triangle, pull the tip slightly to the back and sew together.
For the **Tail Fin** cast on 15 sts to one dpn and purl one row on wrong side. Bind off 1 st at beginning of

next 2 rows, 4 sts at beginning of next 2 rows. Over the remaining 5 sts work 15 rows in St st. Then cast on 4 sts at beginning of next 2 rows and 1 st at beginning of next 2 rows = 15 sts on needle. Knit one row, then bind off all sts. Fold the Tail Fin in half and sew together.

Felting and Finishing:
Sew back seam of slipper. Sew on all the flippers and fins. Felt the slippers in the washing machine, pull in shape, and let dry. Glue on the blue crystals for the eyes.

Slippers with Cuff
Size: Adult 8/9 (9/10) 10/11

Materials:
Approx 200 g felting yarn in purple (100% Wool, Yardage = 50 m/50 g), 1 crochet hook size 7 mm (US L-11), 2 iron-on rhinestone appliqués

Gauge single crochet: Before felting approx 11 sts and 12 rows = 10 x 10 cm/4 x 4". After felting approx 14 sts and 18 rows = 10 x 10 cm/4 x 4".

How to:
Step 1: For the Toe work following the Basic Course on pages 116–117, work 8 sc in a yarn ring 8 sc, join the rnd with slip st in the 1st st. On the 2nd rnd work 2 sc in each st. On the following rnds follow the Basic Instructions working the increases up to the 5th rnd = 26 (28) 30 sts. Cont to work even in sc.
Step 2: For the Instep, after 12 (14) 14 rnds from beg, on the following wrong side rnd work 2 sc in the 8th (9th) 10th st and in the 7th to last (8th to last) 9th to last st. Rep these increase in the same place every 2nd rnd twice more = 32 (34) 36 sts. After 16 (18) 18 rnds from beg (= after a right side rnd) fasten off and determine the center st of the Instep. On the following wrong side row, join yarn from inside after the center st and work 31 (33) 35 sc—the center st remains unworked. After 24 (26) 28 rows from beg, for the Instep work 2 sc in the

11th (12th) 13th st and 11th to last (12th to last) 13th to last st. Repeat these increases in the same place every row 1 (2) 2 times more = 35 (39) 41 sts. Step 3: Work the Cap over 9 sts and 12 (14) 14 rows. Step 4: For the Cuff work sc around top edge. Turn work and work 15 rnds in sc from the inside. Fasten off.

Felting and Finishing:
Felt the slippers in the washing machine, pull in shape, and let dry. Fold Cuff in half to outside and iron on the rhinestones.

Ballerinas with Straps
Size: Child 8/8½ (Adult 7/8) Adult 9/10

Materials:
150 g felting yarn in blue (100% Wool, Yardage = 50 m/50 g), 1 crochet hook size 7 mm (US L-11), 12 rhinestones

Gauge single crochet: Before felting approx 11 sts and 12 rows = 10 x 10 cm/4 x 4". After felting approx 14 sts and 18 rows = 10 x 10 cm/4 x 4".

How to:
Right Ballerina: Step 1: For the Toe follow the Basic Course on pages 116–117 until there are 24 (26) 28 sts, and do not work increases on rnds 3, 5 and 7. Step 2: After 10 (12) 12 rnds from beg (= after a right side rnd) fasten off and determine the center st of the Instep. On the following wrong side row join yarn again from the inside after the center st leave 2 sts worked, then join yarn and work 19 (21) 23 sc and leave the 2 sts before the center st unworked. On the following right side row, for the Foot Opening work the first 2 sts and last 2 sts together = 17 (19) 21 sts. For the Strap, after 12 (14) 18 rows from beg, ch 16 (18) 20 work 1 sc over all 33 (37) 41 sts on the wrong side. On the following right side

row, for the button loop, work to the last 4 sts, ch 2, skip 2 sts, work to end. On the following wrong side row work over all sts, work 2 sc into ch-2 sp. Then leave the Strap sts unworked. After 18 (22) 26 rows from beg, for the Instep work 2 sc in the 4th (5th) 6th st and the 4th to last (5th to last) 6th to last st. Rep these increases in the same place every row 1 (1) 2 times more = 21 (23) 27 sts.
Step 3: Work the Cap over 7 (7) 9 sts and 10 (12) 14 rows.
Step 4: For the finished edge, work sc along top edge of Straps. To form the transition to the Strap work 2 sc together, in the corner of the Strap work 3 sc in 1 st.
Left Ballerina: Work same as right Ballerina, reversing the Straps as follows: After 12 (14) 18 rows from beg, with an extra strand of yarn, join to the 1st st and ch 16 (18) 20, then fasten off. Complete the Ballerina in reverse.
Felting and Finishing:
Felt the Ballerinas in the washing machine, pull in shape, and let dry. Attach rhinestones on the Straps.

The Gauge

Before making a project, it is recommended to work a gauge swatch. In this way you can check to see if you are getting the suggested stitch and row gauge. If the swatch is smaller, then use more stitches or try working with larger needles. If it is larger, then use fewer stitches or try smaller needles.

1. Stockinette Stitch
A Stockinette Stitch swatch tends to curl at the edges after felting; the border is no longer smooth. However, when the pieces are sewn together, it is no longer a problem.

2. Garter Stitch
A felted garter stitch swatch is smaller, thicker and denser than a Stockinette swatch with the same number of stitches and rows.
.

3. Seed Stitch
A seed stitch swatch felts the most evenly in both stitches and rows. Therefore it is a particularly well-suited stitch for felting.

Warm Feet in Pink
for the Little Ones...

Felted slippers in pink are popular with both big and little ladies. For adults, the color blocking in pink and orange—with a small rose detail—gives vivid style.

... & Big Ones

For children, these slippers can be a bit playful. You can attach ribbons, flaps, or flowers. The shades you choose can be tone on tone, or brightly colorful.

Child's Slippers with Cuff
Size: Child 6½/7 (7½/8) 8/8½

Materials:

Approx 100 (150) 150 g felting yarn in pink (100% Wool, Yardage = 50 m/50 g), approx 50 g felting yarn in pink-purple-orange mix, 1 crochet hook size 7 mm (US L-11)

Gauge single crochet: Before felting approx 11 sts and 12 rows = 10 x 10 cm/4 x 4". After felting approx 14 sts and 18 rows = 10 x 10 cm/4 x 4".

How to:

Step 1: For the Toe work following the Basic Course on pages 116–117 with pink, work 8 sc in a yarn ring, join the rnd with slip st in the 1st st. On the 2nd rnd work 2 sc in each st. On the following rnds follow the Basic Course working the increases until there are 20 (20) 22 sts. Cont to work even in sc.

Step 2: For the Instep, after 8 (10) 10 rnds from beg, on the following wrong side rnd work 2 sc in the 7th (7th) 8th st and in the 6th to last (6th to last) 7th to last st. Rep these increase in the same place every 2nd rnd once more = 24 (24) 26 sts. After 12 (14) 14 rnds from beg (= after a right side rnd) fasten off and determine the center st of the Instep. On the following wrong side row, join yarn from inside in the 2nd st after the center st and work 21 (21) 23 sc—the center 3 sts remain unworked. For the Foot opening, on the following 2nd row, work the first 2 and last 2 sts together = 19 (19) 21 sts. After 16 (18) 18 rows/rnds from beg, for the Instep work 2 sc in the 6th (6th) 7th st and 6th to last 6th to last) 7th

to last st. Repeat these increases in the same place every 2nd row once more = 23 (23) 25 sts.

Step 3: Work the Cap over 7 sts and 12 (12) 14 rows.

Step 4: For the Cuff with pink work sc around top edge as described in the Basic Course for 2 rnds, then work 1 rnd (right side rnd) through back loops only. Then for the flap, with pink-purple-orange mix work 7 rows sc, working through the front loops and leaving the center front st unworked, at the same time, inc 1 sc each side every 2nd row twice. Fasten off.

Work 2nd slipper in same way.

Felting and Finishing:

Felt the slippers in the washing machine, pull in shape, and let dry. (See pages 34–35 for Basic Felting Instructions.)

Child's Slippers with Flowers
Size: Child 6/6½ (6½/7) 7½/8

Materials:

Approx 100 (150) 150 g felting yarn in pink-purple-orange mix, 1 crochet hook size 7 mm (US L-11), 2 orange buttons 1 cm/¼" in diameter

Flower: Make a yarn ring and work as follows:

Rnd 1: Ch 1, *1 sc in ring, ch 1; rep from * 5 times more, end with 1 slip st in 1st sc.

Rnd 2: In each ch-1 sp work 1 sl st, ch 2, 1 dc, 1 tr, 1 dc, ch 2 and 1 sl st, end with 1 sl st in 1st st.

Gauge single crochet: Before felting approx 11 sts and 12 rows = 10 x 10 cm/4 x 4". After felting approx 14 sts and 18 rows = 10 x 10 cm/4 x 4".

How to:

Step 1: For the Toe work following the Basic Course on pages 116–117, work 8 sc in a yarn ring, join the rnd with slip st in the 1st st. On the 2nd rnd work 2 sc in each st. On the following rnds follow the Basic Course working the increases until there are 18 (20) 20 sts. Cont to work even in sc.

Step 2: For the Instep, after 8 (8) 10 rnds from beg, on the following wrong side rnd work 2 sc in the 6th (7th) 7th st and in the 5th to last (6th to last) 6th to last st. Rep these increases in the same place every 2nd rnd 0 (1) 1 time more = 20 (24) 24 sts. After 10 (12) 14 rnds from beg (= after a right side rnd) fasten off and determine the center st of the Instep. On the following wrong side row, join yarn

from inside in the 2nd st after the center st and work 17 (21) 21 sc—the center 3 sts remain un-worked. For the Foot opening, in the following 2nd row, work the first 2 and last 2 sts together every 2nd row 1 (1) 2 times = 15 (17) 17 sts. After 16 (16) 18 rows/rnds from beg, for the Instep work 2 sc in the 5th st and 5th to last st. Repeat these increases in the same place every 2nd row once more = 19 (21) 21 sts.

Step 3: Work the Cap over 5 (7) 7 sts and 10 rows.

Step 4: For the Cuff work sc around top edge as described in the Basic Course.

Work 2nd slipper in same way.

Felting and Finishing:

Crochet two flowers. Felt the slippers and flowers in the washing machine, pull in shape, and let dry. (See pages 34–35 for Basic Felting Instructions.) Sew flower and button to slipper (see photo).

Baby Booties
Size: Child 5/6 (6/6½)

Materials:
Approx 100 g felting yarn in coral mix and 50 g in coral, 1 crochet hook size 7 mm (US L-11), 2 small white flower buttons, 30 cm/12" orange-white plaid ribbon, 6 mm wide

Gauge single crochet: Before felting approx 11 sts and 12 rows = 10 x 10 cm/4 x 4". After felting approx 14 sts and 18 rows = 10 x 10 cm/4 x 4".

How to:
Step 1: For the Toe work following the Basic Course on pages 116–117 with coral mix, work 8 sc in a yarn ring, join the rnd with slip st in the 1st st. On the 2nd rnd work 2 sc in each st. On the following rnds follow the Basic Course working the increases until there are 18 sts. Cont to work even in sc.
Step 2: For the Instep, after 6 (8) rnds from beg, on the following wrong side rnd work 2 sc in the 6th st and in the 5th to last st = 20 sts. After 8 (10) rnds from beg (= after a right side rnd) fasten off and determine the center st of the Instep. On the follow-

ing wrong side row, join yarn from inside after the center st and work 19 sc—the center st remains unworked. After 14 (16) rows from beg, for the Instep work 2 sc in the 16th st and 6th to last st. Repeat these increases in the same place every row 0 (1) time more = 21 (23) sts.
Step 3: Work the Cap over 5 sts and 10 (12) rows.
Step 4: For the Cuff work sc around top edge with coral mix as described in the Basic Course for 7 rounds, turning the work at end of every rnd. With coral work 2 more rnds and 1 rnd crab st (work sc from left to right). Fasten off.
Work 2nd Bootie in same way.

Felting and Finishing:
Felt the slippers in the washing machine, pull in shape and let dry. (See pages 34–35 for Basic Felting Instructions.) Fold Cuff in half to outside. Cut ribbon in half, tie in a bow, and attach to bootie with button (see photo).

Slippers with Rose Motif
Size: Adult 8/9

Materials:
150 g felting yarn in pink (100% Wool, Yardage = 50 m/50 g), small amount in orange, 1 circular needle size 8 mm (US 11), 1 set (5) dpn size 8 mm (US 11), piece of orange felt, 2 brooch pins, fabric glue

Gauge Stockinette Stitch: Before felting 11 sts and 16 rows = 10 x 10 cm/4 x 4". After felting 15 sts and 24 rows = 10 x 10 cm/4 x 4".

How to:
With circular needle, cast on 30 sts with pink and work in Stockinette st for 34 rows. Then divide the sts over 4 dpn and join to work in rounds, and on the 1st round, increase 1 stitch at beginning and end of round = 32 sts. Then work 15 rounds. Change to orange and work 5 rounds. For the **Toe**, work k2tog with the last 2 sts of the 1st and 3rd needles, and the first 2 sts of the 2nd and 4th needle every rnd 6 times, and after 3 decrease rounds have been worked, complete the toe with

pink. Cut yarn and draw through 8 sts and secure. Work a 2nd slipper in same way.

Felting and Finishing:
Sew back seam of slipper. Felt the slippers in the washing machine, pull in shape, and let dry. (See pages 34–35 for Basic Felting Instructions.)

Rose Motifs:
For each rose cut the felt into a strip 4–5 cm/1½-2" wide and 30 cm/12" long and a circle approx 5 cm/2" in diameter. Fold the strip in half and form a spiral starting with the open edge in the middle, and glue to the circle. Trim the edges of the circle and glue the rose to a brooch pin. Attach the roses to the front of each slipper.

With the Right Spin

The innovative ideas for knitting socks are seemingly inexhaustible. It is possible to knit a sock in spiral form without working the classic heel.

With this type of sock, the spiral technique is used for the entire sock or for the Heel width. Thus, the shape adapts to the entire Foot and around the Heel, without the conventional knitted-in Heel. This is the perfect method for those who find knitting the heel difficult.

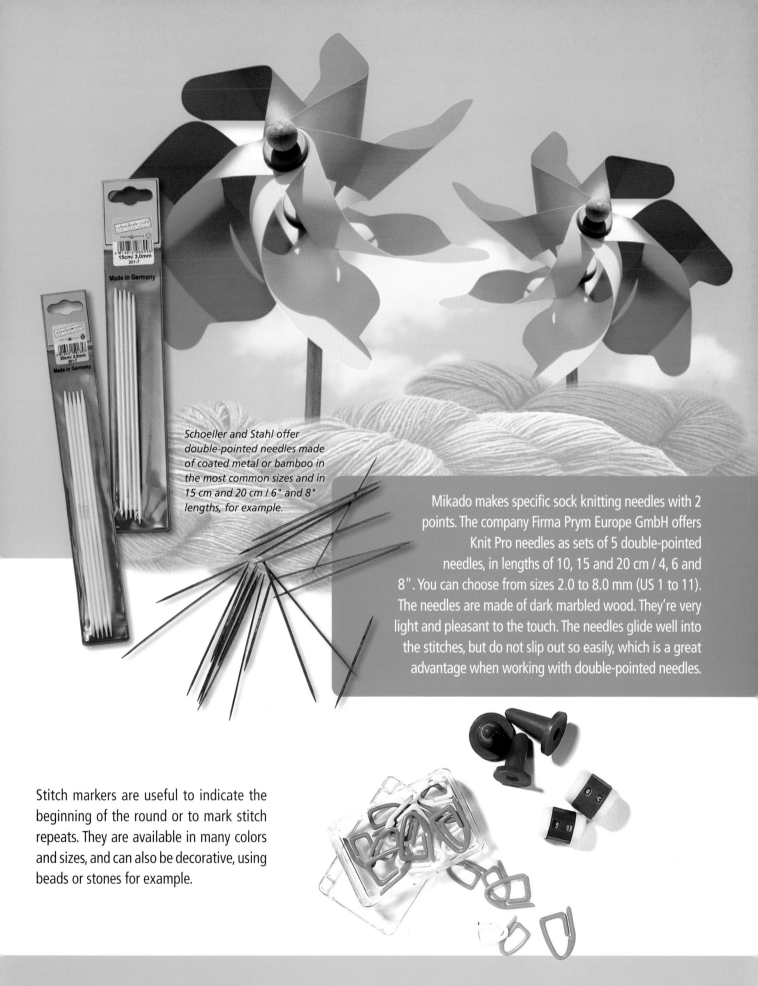

Schoeller and Stahl offer double-pointed needles made of coated metal or bamboo in the most common sizes and in 15 cm and 20 cm / 6" and 8" lengths, for example.

Mikado makes specific sock knitting needles with 2 points. The company Firma Prym Europe GmbH offers Knit Pro needles as sets of 5 double-pointed needles, in lengths of 10, 15 and 20 cm / 4, 6 and 8". You can choose from sizes 2.0 to 8.0 mm (US 1 to 11). The needles are made of dark marbled wood. They're very light and pleasant to the touch. The needles glide well into the stitches, but do not slip out so easily, which is a great advantage when working with double-pointed needles.

Stitch markers are useful to indicate the beginning of the round or to mark stitch repeats. They are available in many colors and sizes, and can also be decorative, using beads or stones for example.

Basic Course for: **Spiral Socks**

The Spiral Sock is always worked "straight" from the Cuff, and over knit 4, purl 4 ribbing over 4 rounds = 1 Pattern repeat (rep). After setting up this pattern, shift it 1 stitch to the left (every 4 rows = 1 Spiral-Pattern set). Therefore, the knitted tube is rotated in a spiral. You can use the stitch numbers given on the Size Table on pages 142/143.

The stitch number must always be a multiple of 4 (so that there is always an even number of stitches on each needle).

Since the spiral is extremely flexible, more sizes can be used for the same number of sts. The number of stitches and spiral pattern depends on the type of sock or the length of the Leg and shoe size.

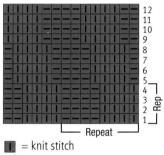

Repeat

Rep

■ = knit stitch
– = purl stitch

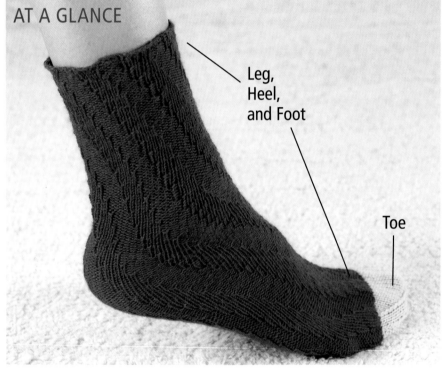

AT A GLANCE

Leg, Heel, and Foot

Toe

Leg, Heel, Foot

The spiral consists of the Leg, Heel, and Foot. Cast on stitches following the Size Table. Next work the desired border. Then continue in the spiral pattern repeat. Since the Sock turns after a few repeats, mark the orientation at the beginning with a marker, such as a safety pin. This marker is carried along with the knitting. Remove it only when you have the second set directly above it. In this way, the beginning of the round is always recognizable.

Leg, Heel, and Foot...

...with Toe.

The sock is finished!

After the spiral, follow the Basic Instructions for the Toe Band in knit stitches (= Stockinette St), unless otherwise indicated. On the 1st and 3rd needles knit the third and second to last stitches together, on the 2nd and 4th needle work SKP with the 2nd and 3rd stitches. Repeat these decreases every 2nd round, until the stitch number is halved. Then continue decreases every round until there are 8 stitches. Cut yarn and draw it through remaining stitches and secure.

Once the socks are finished, you will understand why they are called spiral socks: you will see a spiral tube is very elastic. You can make this "tube" even more appealing by using different colors, for example, use another color for the Cuff and Toe, or work a different pattern stitch on the Cuff, such as a Rolled Edge, or one with a fancy yarn. Other great effects are created with fringe, pompon or glitter yarns. In addition, you can decorate the Leg and Cuff with buttons or beads.

Toe Band

Finished Spiral Sock

Socks with Spiral Heel

Cast on the number of stitches according to the Size Table, which will always be a multiple of 4 (= in order to have an even number of sts on each needle). Work the Leg in the desired pattern and length. (Note that the total stitch count must be divisible by 4.) Here you are only knitting the Heel as a spiral. The number of pattern sets for the appropriate size is indicated in the specific instructions. You can work the Foot in Stockinette Stitch, and use a multicolored yarn for a more decorative look. For single color yarns, it looks nice when the pattern used on the Leg continues into the Foot. It is best to continue the pattern only on the top side of the Foot (2nd and 3rd needles) and work the bottom of the Foot in Stockinette stitch (1st and 4th needles). At the end, after the desired foot length, work the Toe Band in Stockinette Stitch or as specified in the instructions.

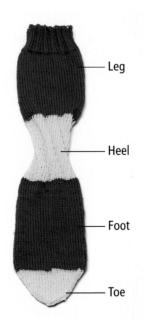

Leg

Heel

Foot

Toe

All-around Winners

The stitch pattern spirals along with the spiralling of the socks. The back side view, at right, shows you how snug these socks are without a knit-in heel.

The two socks you see here are shown from the rear view. You can see how the pattern continues to spiral around the feet, shaping to the form of your feet.

Colorful Striped Socks
Size: Adult 9/10

Materials:
Approx 100 g each of sock yarn in green and self-striping (75% Wool, 25% Polyamide, Yardage = 210 m/50 g), 1 set (5) dpn size 2.5 mm (US 1)

How to:
For the Rolled Edge with green cast on 56 stitches (= 14 sts per needle) and work 15 rounds in Stockinette st. On the last round decrease 4 .stitches evenly over each needle (= 40 stitches). Then for the Leg work in Stripe Pattern as follows: Rnd 1: With green, *k1, k1 in row below; rep from * around. Rnd 2: With self-striping yarns, *k1 in row below, k1; rep from * around. Rep rnds 1 and 2 for 12 cm/4¾". On the next round inc 4 stitches evenly on each needle (= 56 stitches). Then for the Spiral-Heel with self-striping yarn, work 11 Spiral-Pattern sets, shifting the pattern 1 stitch to the left (see Basic Course on pages 132–133). After the Spiral-Heel decrease 4 stitches evenly over each needle (= 40 stitches). Cont to rep rounds 1 and 2 of pattern of the Leg for 13 cm/5". Increase 4 stitches evenly over each needle (= 56 stitches). Work the Band Toe in Stockinette Stitch with green.
Work a second sock in same way.

Socks with Picot Edge
Size: Adult 10/11

Materials:
Approx 100 g sock yarn in green and 50 g in natural (75% Wool, 18% Polyamide, 7% Acrylic, Yardage = 210 m/50 g), 1 set (5) dpn size 2.5 mm (US 1)

How to:
With natural, cast on 56 stitches (= 14 stitches per needle) and work picot edge as follows: Work 10 rounds in Stockinette St. On next rnd, *knit 2 together, yo; rep from * around. Then work another 10 rounds in Stockinette st. Then fold the first 10 rounds to inside and knit 1st st on needle together with corresponding cast-on st, continue across row in this way until all cast-on stitches are joined to the sts on the needle. With green work 1 Spiral-Pattern set, following the Basic Instructions on page 132–133. Then work in Spiral-Pattern sets working the Openwork Pat following the Stitch Chart. Rep rnds 1–16 of the Stitch Chart sets. When 34 Spiral-Pattern sets have been worked, work the Band Toe in Stockinette Stitch.
Work a second sock in same way.

Stitch Chart

Repeat (rows numbered 1–16)

Stitch Key

U	= yo
I	= 1 k st
—	= 1 p st
⊿	= knit 2 sts together
＞	= knit 2 sts together through back loops

Children's Socks
Size: Child 6½/7

Materials:
50 g fuchsia (80% Wool, 20% Polyamide, Yardage = approx 155 m/50 g), 1 set (5) double-pointed needles (dpn) 2.5 – 3 mm (US 1 – 3)

Main Pat: Knit tightly!
Rnd 1: *knit 2, purl 2 sts; rep from * around.
Rnd 2 and all even-numbered rnds: Knit the k sts and purl the p sts.
On every odd-numbered rnd, shift the pattern 1 st to the left, that is:
Rnd 3: *Knit 1, purl 2, knit 1; rep from *.
Rnd 5: *Purl 2, knit 2; rep from *.
Rnd 7: *Purl 1, knit 2 purl 1; rep from *.
Cont shifting sts in this way.

Gauge, in Main Pat: 28 sts and 36 rows = 10 x 10 cm/4 x 4".

How to:
Cast on 40 sts, divide sts evenly over 4 needles (= 10 sts per needle) and join to work in rounds. Work in Main Pat. After 28 cm/11" from beg, beg with the Toe. On the following rnd, work all purl 2 sts together maintaining the spiral = 30 sts. Work 7 rnds even. On the next rnd work all knit 2 sts together, maintaining the spiral = 20 sts. Work 3 rnds even. On the following rnd work k2tog around = 10 sts. Work 1 rnd even. On the following rnd work k2tog around = 5 sts. Cut yarn, draw through remaining sts and secure.
Work a second sock in same way.

Women's Socks
Size: Adult 9/10

Materials:
Approx 100 g Ecru (80% Wool, 20% Polyamide, Yardage = approx 155 m/50 g), 1 set (5) double-pointed needles (dpn) size 2.5 – 3 mm (US 1 – 3)

Main Pat: Knit tightly!
Rnd 1: *Knit 2, purl 2; rep from * around.
Rnd 2 rnds and all even-numbered rnds: Knit the k sts and purl the p sts.
On every odd-numbered rnd, shift the pattern 1 st to the left, that is:
Rnd 3: *Knit 1, purl 2, knit 1; rep from *.
Rnd 5: *Purl 2, knit 2; rep from *.
Rnd 7: *Purl 1, knit 2, purl 1; rep from *.
Cont shifting sts in this way.

Gauge, in Main Pat: 28 sts and 36 rows = 10 x 10 cm/4 x 4".

How to:
Cast on 56 sts and divide sts evenly over 4 needles (= 14 sts per needle) and join to work in rounds. Work in Main Pat. After 39 cm/15½" from cast on, begin the Toe as follows: On the following rnd, work all purl 2 sts together maintaining the spiral = 42 sts. Work 9 rnds even in pattern. On the next rnd work all knit 2 sts together, maintaining the spiral = 28 sts. Work 5 rnds even. On the next rnd work k2tog around = 14 sts. Work 3 rnds even. On the next rnd work k2tog around = 7 sts. Cut yarn, draw through remaining sts and secure.
Work a second sock in same way.

What Comes Around!

Pompons, rolls, or cuffs—
How you embellish their Spiral Socks
and what color to choose is
all up to you.

The spiral pattern has an interesting surface texture. It offers enough of a decorative contrast to cuffs and toes worked in different colors or stitch patterns. The socks in the pastel stripe pattern have an edge decorated with pompon yarn.

The colors in the narrow stripes at the toe are repeated on the distinctive rolled edges of the cuff. This is a beautiful addition to solid-color socks.

Socks with Rolled Edges
Size: Adult 9/10

Materials:
Approx 50 g each in yellow and red, 100 g in orange (75% Wool, 18% Polyamide, 7% Acrylic, Yardage = 210 m/50 g), two sets (5 per set) of double-pointed needles (dpn) size 2.5 mm (US 1)

How to:
With yellow, cast on 56 stitches (= 14 stitches per needle) and for the 1st Rolled Edge work 24 rounds in Stockinette st. For the 2nd Rolled Edge, with the 2nd set of dpn and orange, cast on 56 stitches and work 22 rounds in Stockinette st. Then place the 2nd Rolled Edge over the 1st Rolled Edge and with orange, knit 1 stitch from each needle tog until all

stitches are joined, then knit 1 round. For the 3rd Rolled Edge with red, cast on 56 stitches and work 20 rounds in Stockinette st. Then place this Rolled Edge over the other two and with red knit 1 stitch from each needle tog until all stitches are joined on one needle, then knit 1 round. Then with orange work 26 Spiral-Pattern sets, shifting the pattern 1 stitch to the left (see Basic Course on pages 132–133). Work the Toe Band in Stockinette Stitch, alternating 2 rounds in yellow, orange, and red.

Socks with Pompons
Size: 8/9

Materials:
Approx 50 g each natural white, yellow and rose (75% Wool, 25% Polyamide, Yardage = 210 m/50 g), 200 g yellow-rose-natural white pompon yarn (100% Polyester, Yardage = 100 m/200 g), 1 set (5) dpn size 2.5 mm (US 1), 1 sewing needle

How to:
With yellow cast on 56 stitches (= 14 stitches per needle) and work 1 Spiral-Pattern set following the Basic Course on pages 132–133. Then work 1 Pattern set in rose and 1 Pattern set in white—every Pattern set shift 1 stitch to the left. Cont in Stripe Pat as established until there are 34 Spiral-Pattern

sets. Then work the Toe Band in Stockinette Stitch with rose following the Basic Course on pages 132–133. Along the cast-on edges, work 14 stitches with the pompon yarn, that is: In the first 4 knit stitches work 2 knit sts with the pompon yarn, over the 4 purl stitches push up a pompon. Continue in the way to work 2 knit sts over the 4 knit sts and a pompon on the purl stitches. Because the stitches cannot be bound off, sew the open stitches to the underlying stitches.

Socks with Cuffs
Size: Adult 9/10

Materials:
Approx 100 g each yellow and white (75% Wool, 25% Polyamide, Yardage = 210 m/50 g), 1 set (5) dpn size 2.5 mm (US 1)

How to:
With white cast on 56 stitches (= 14 stitches per needle). For the Cuff work 40 rows in Ribbing Pat (= knit 4, purl 4). Change to yellow and work 35 Spi-

ral-Pattern sets, always shifting 1 stitch to the left, as described in the Basic Course on pages 132–133. Then work the Toe Band in white and Stockinette st.

Toe Variations for all

The Star Toe

The Propeller

❶ For the Star Toe you will need an even number of stitches per needle. Extra stitches will have already been evenly distributed and decreased if necessary in the previous rounds. With the Star Toe two stitches are decreased per needle. The numbers for the Star Toe can be found on the Size Table (see page 142). It specifies how many rows are knit to the first decrease round. On the decrease rounds, the number of stitches that are worked before each decrease is stated in the Table.

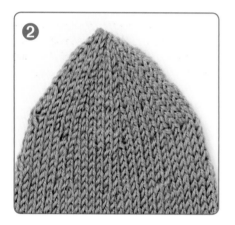

❷ If the Star Toe number is 7, then work 6 rows without decreases. On the first decrease round work every 6th and 7th stitches together. The number of sts on the needle between the decreases is the number of following rounds to work without decreases. In this example there are 5 stitches, followed by 5 rounds without decreases. Then comes the second decrease round, and knit every 5th and 6th stitches together. Between the decreases there are 4 stitches, also followed by 4 rounds without decreases.

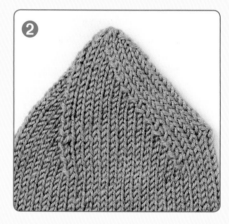

❸ Continue in this way until there are 2 stitches per needle, or 8 stitches in total. Draw a double strand through these stitches, pull together tightly, and secure. The Star Toe looks smooth.

Knitted Socks

Toe

The Spiral Toe

❶ This Toe is very easy to make and is great for beginners. In every 2nd round the 1st and 2nd stitches of each needle are knit together. If only a third of the original number of stitches are on the needles, then the decreases are worked on every round.

❶ A nice variation of the classic toe is the Spiral Toe. It is easy to knit and is durable. On every 2nd round work SKP with the 2nd and 3rd stitches on each needle. That is, slip the 2nd stitch, knit the 3rd stitch and pass the slipped stitch over the knit stitch.

❷ Continue the decreases until there are 2 stitches per needle, or 8 stitches in total. Draw a double strand through these stitches, pull together tightly and secure.

❷ Continue these decreases until there are 2 stitches per needle, or 8 stitches in total. Draw a double strand through these stitches, pull together tightly, and secure.

❸ These decreases form a propeller shape which is how this toe style got its name. It is more suitable for a tapered foot.

❸ Viewing the toe from the top, you can see how the decreases form a spiral. This toe shape is a good one for wearing with shoes.

Size Table for **Standard Socks**

Gauge with 2–3 mm (US 1–3) needles in Stockinette St: 28 sts and 40 rows/rnds = 10 x 10 cm/4 x 4"

Size	child 5/6	child 6/6½	child 6½/7	child 7½/8	child 8/8½	child 9/9½	adult 7-8	adult 8-9	adult 9-10	adult 10/11	adult 11/12	adult 14	adult 15
foot length in cm/in	14.5/5¾	16/6¼	17.5/6¾	18.5/7¼	20/7¾	21.5/8½	22.5/8¾	24/9½	25.5/10	26.5/10½	28/11	29.5/11½	30.5/12
cast on stitches	44	48	48	52	52	56	56	60	60	64	64	68	72
Heel Cap													
heel flap width	22	24	24	26	26	28	28	30	30	32	32	34	36
rows in heel flap	20	22	22	24	24	26	26	28	28	30	30	32	34
stitch number for cap	8	8	8	8	8	10	10	10	10	10	10	12	12
number of stitches decreased each side	11	12	12	13	13	14	14	15	15	16	16	17	18
Boomerang Heel													
Heel stitches of Boomerang Heel	7/8/7	8/8/8	8/8/8	8/10/8	8/10/8	9/10/9	9/10/9	10/10/10	10/10/10	10/12/10	10/12/10	11/12/11	12/12/12
4-Step Heel													
heel flap width	22	24	24	26	26	28	28	30	30	32	32	34	36
rows to 1st step	8	10	10	12	12	14	14	16	16	18	18	20	22
sts on hold each side	3	4	4	5	5	6	6	7	7	8	8	9	10
rows to 2nd step	6	8	8	10	10	12	12	16	16	18	18	20	22
dec sts each side	3	4	4	5	5	6	6	8	8	9	9	10	11
rows to end of heel	6	8	8	10	10	12	12	14	14	16	16	18	20
decrease gusset stitches each side	4	5	5	6	6	7	7	8	8	9	9	10	11
foot length from center heel to start of toe	11	12	13.5	14.5	16	17	18	19	20.5	21	22.5	24	24.5
Star Toe numbers	5	6	6	6	6	7	7	7	7	8	8	8	9

Size Table for **Socks with 2 circular needles**

Gauge: 30 stitches and 42 rows/rounds = 10 x 10 cm/4 x 4"

Size	child 4/5	child 5/6	child 6/6½	child 6½/7	child 7½/8	child 8/8½	child 9/9½	adult 7-8	adult 8-9	adult 9-10	adult 10/11	adult 11/12	adult 14	adult 15
total foot length cm/in	13.5/5½	14.5/5¾	16/6¼	17.5/6¾	18.5/7¼	20/8	21.5/8½	22.5/8¾	24/9½	25.5/10	26.5/10½	28/11	29.5/11½	30.5/12
cast on stitches	40	44	48	48	52	52	56	56	60	60	64	64	68	72
heel flap width in sts	20	22	24	24	26	26	28	28	30	30	32	32	34	36
heel flap height in rows	20	22	24	24	26	26	28	28	30	30	32	32	34	36
number of stitches for the cap	8	8	8	8	10	10	10	10	10	10	12	12	12	12
number of decrease stitches each side	11	12	13	13	14	14	15	15	16	16	17	17	18	19
foot length to start of toe in cm/in	10.5/4¼	11/4½	12/4¾	13.5/5½	14.5/5¾	16/6¼	17/6½	18/7	19/7½	20.5/8	21/8¼	22.5/8¾	24/9½	24.5/9½

Size Table for **Socks Knit from the Toe Up**

Gauge with 2–3 mm (US 1–3) needles in Stockinette Stitch: 28 sts and 40 rows/rounds = 10 x 10 cm/4 x 4"

Size	child 4/5	child 5/6	child 6/6½	child 6½/7	child 7½/8	child 8/8½	child 9/9½	adult 7-8	adult 8-9	adult 9-10	adult 10/11	adult 11/12	adult 14	adult 15
sock length in cm/in	13.5/5½	14.5/5¾	16/6¼	17.5/6¾	19/7½	20/7¾	21.5/8½	23/9	24.5/9½	25.5/10	27/10½	28/11	29/11½	30.5/12
stitch number for instep and sole	38	42	46	46	50	50	54	54	58	58	62	62	66	66
from toe to start of instep in cm/in	8/3½	9/3½	10.5/4¼	12/4¾	13.5/5½	14.5/5¾	15.5/6	17/6½	18/7	19/7½	20/8	21/8¼	22/8½	23/9
number of increases for the instep and heel	3	3	4	4	5	5	6	6	7	7	8	8	9	9
stitch number of the cap	9	9	11	11	13	13	15	15	17	17	19	19	21	21
number of decreases on right and left of the cap	5	5	7	7	9	9	11	11	13	13	15	15	17	17
stitch number for the leg	38	42	46	46	50	50	54	54	58	58	62	62	66	66

Size Table for **Crocheted Socks**

Gauge with 2.5 mm (US B/1) hook and hdc: 23 hdc and 18 rows/rounds = 10 x 10 cm/4 x 4"

Size	child 4/5	child 5/6	child 6/6½	child 6½/7	child 7½/8	child 8/8½	child 9/9½	adult 7-8	adult 8-9	adult 9-10	adult 10/11	adult 11/12	adult 14	adult 15
Sock length in cm/in	13.5/5½	14.5/5¾	16/6¼	17.5/6¾	19/7½	20/7¾	21.5/8½	23/9	24.5/9½	25.5/10	27/10½	28/11	29/11½	30.5/12
stitch numbers for instep and sole	24	28	28	32	32	36	36	40	40	44	44	48	48	52
from toe to start of instep heel in cm/in	7	8	9.5	11	12.5	13.5	14.5	16	17	18	19	20	21	22
number of increases for the instep and heel	3	3	4	4	4	5	5	5	6	6	6	7	7	7
number of stitches after increase in instep and heel	36	40	44	48	48	56	56	60	64	68	68	76	76	80
number of stitches for the cap	9	9	11	11	11	13	13	13	15	15	15	17	17	17
number of rows in cap	9	9	13	13	13	15	15	15	19	19	19	21	21	21
number of decreases with start of leg	1	1	1	1	1	2	2	2	2	2	2	3	3	3
number of stitches for the leg	24	28	28	32	32	36	36	40	40	44	44	48	48	52

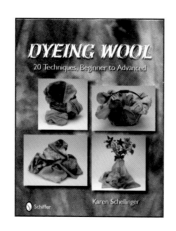

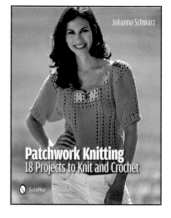